THE BLACK BOOK

Universal's Guide to

Uniform Legal Citations

THE BLACK BOOK

Universal's Guide to

Uniform Legal Citations

Meera Kaura Patel

B.A. English (Hons.) (University of Delhi)
LL.B. (Campus Law Centre, University of Delhi)
LL.M. (University of Ottawa, Canada)

Universal
Law Publishing Co. Pvt. Ltd.
NEW DELHI - INDIA

2011 Edition

ISBN : 978-81-7534-993-3

Published by
UNIVERSAL LAW PUBLISHING CO. PVT. LTD.
C-FF-1A, Dilkhush Industrial Estate,
(Near Azadpur Metro Station) G.T. Karnal Road,
Delhi-110 033
Tel : 011-27438103, 27215334, 42381334
Fax : 011-27458529
E-mail *(For sales inquiries)* : sales@unilawbooks.com
E-mail *(For editorial inquiries)* : edit@unilawbooks.com
Website : www.unilawbooks.com

Recommended citation: *Universal's Guide to Uniform Legal Citations,* Meera Kaura Patel (New Delhi: Universal Law Publishing Co. Pvt. Ltd., 2011)

Computer Typeset at Aesthetic & *Printed* at Taj Press, New Delhi.

ACKNOWLEDGMENTS

I wish to thank my publishers, Universal Law Publishing Co. Pvt. Ltd. for giving me this opportunity to undertake the herculean task of compiling a uniform guide for legal citations. The manuscript would not have seen the light of the day without the blessings of my Guru Shri Sai Baba. I am indebted to my husband Mr. Tejas Patel, Associate, Clifford Chance LL.P. for helpful suggestions and comments. I am grateful to Mr. Ramesh Gupta, Senior Advocate, Prof. Nomita Agarwal, my son Agustya Patel, my family, friends and associates for constant support and encouragement. I would also like to thank my research assistant Gaurav Goyal, student, IP University, for his assistance in compiling the list of abbreviations of Indian Legal Periodicals and Indian Journals.

PREFACE

Organizing legal citations in the form of footnotes, endnotes and bibliography was once only considered a part of legal academic writing. Legal citations are, however, extensively used by corporate law firms while preparing opinions, memorandums, etc., by government commissions while preparing reports, by lawyers while preparing written submissions, petitions, applications etc., by professors while writing articles, books, etc., by law book publishers and journal publishers while prescribing a citation format for footnotes, endnotes, bibliography etc., and by students while writing legal academic papers, articles, memorandum for moots, etc.

Legal citation is the legal writing practice used to refer and give credit to authoritative sources. In the absence of any uniform way, authors adopt different ways to refer to a source. To avoid such ambiguity, some countries have developed a standard *de facto* citation practice which is now widely followed by most of the academic and legal institutions. For instance:

1. Australia: Australian Guide to Legal Citation (AGLC) is the standard citation format in 27 law journals approximately.
2. Canada: Canadian Guide to Uniform Legal Citation (McGill Guide) is the standard citation format across all the law schools and legal journals in Canada.
3. United Kingdom: The Oxford Standard for Citation of Legal Authorities (OSCOLA) has been adopted as the standard citation format by various prestigious journals and the courts.
4. United States of America: The Bluebook: A Uniform System of Citation, ALWD Citation Manual and Maroonbook are usually followed as the standard citation formats across various law schools, legal journals and courts in USA.

However, no such uniform practice existed in India. Most of the prestigious journals follow other foreign citation formats. Some law schools and journals prescribe their own citation formats. The authors mostly send their academic works to various journals and publishers with any citation format. It, then, becomes the task of editors to revise and edit all the footnotes or endnotes in addition to the text of the articles, essays or notes. Internationally, whereas, the authors must comply with the uniform legal citation format before their work is accepted for publication. The task of the editors is limited to the editing of the language or the editing of the legal text with the author's permission. The absence of such a process in India results in time consuming editing and delayed publications. Also, works of authors lack a scientific approach in argument formation and research. As a result, the final product (thesis) is more expository or explanatory than analytical or argumentative.

October 2010 **MEERA KAURA PATEL**

THE NEED FOR UNIFORMITY IN THE CITATION FORMAT

In the absence of any uniform practice, a need to prescribe standard rules to refer to authoritative resources was felt by the author. The other advantages of standard legal citation are as following:

1. It enables the readers to identify the relevant resources in others' works aiding their area of research, thereby promoting legal research methodology in India;
2. It encourages the authors to cite the resources in the prescribed format which, if followed uniformly by publishers, will be more reader friendly;
3. Citing works properly will prevent the authors from indulging in plagiarism, thereby promoting innovative ideas amongst legal fraternity;
4. It also gives respect and recognition to other authors for their ideas, thereby protecting their moral rights over their work;
5. It indicates the genuineness, weight and persuasiveness of a source referred/used;
6. Signals used with the citations convey the type and degree of support. It, thus, promotes an academic debate when authors agree or disagree with the ideas of other authors; and
7. Proper citation for an argument or an idea provides evidence that the idea/argument is well researched.

The fact that India is on the verge of opening up its legal services to the international law firms, it is imperative that we develop uniform standard practices which are at par with the international practice.

Universal's Guide to Uniform Legal Citations seeks to address the common concerns of people involved in legal, academic and professional writing.

CONTENTS

1

GENERAL NOTES ON CITATION

FOOTNOTES: RULES

2

LEGISLATION

INDIA

3

CASE-LAW

4
GOVERNMENT DOCUMENTS

5
INTERNATIONAL LAW SOURCES

6

SECONDARY SOURCES

1
GENERAL NOTES ON CITATION

The rules in this Guide apply to footnotes, in-text citations, quotations, bibliographies and endnotes. When an example requires comma, use comma. If a rule states that parentheses "( )" must be used, brackets "[ ]" should not be substituted. If a rule states that double quotes "must be used, single quotes, should not be substituted. When a rule states that *italics* must be used, CAPITAL LETTERS or *underlining* should not be substituted. Similarly, if a rule states that CAPITAL LETTERS or *underlining* should be used, *italics* should not be substituted. It is imperative that the citation rules in Universal's Guide to Uniform Legal Citations should be complied with to achieve uniformity. Universal's Guide to Uniform Legal Citations prescribes different citation formats for books, journal articles, case-laws, government reports, international reports, NGO reports, newspaper reports/articles, electronic resources etc.

FOOTNOTES: RULES

When writing a legal research paper or preparing a memorandum or a report, use of footnotes is encouraged. Use of endnotes is only encouraged for legal essay writing. In legal writing, the two most common forms of footnotes are *textual footnotes* and *citation footnotes*. *Textual footnotes* contain matters of related interest to the subject of writing, but are sufficiently tangential that their presence in the main body of the paper may distract the reader from the thrust of the argument. *Citation footnotes*, on the other hand, are used to indicate the sources from which the author derives the argument or quotation. Pinpointing citation footnotes is very important to avoid plagiarism and to help the reader locate the source/reference. Citation and textual footnotes often inter-change and both can also occur within the same footnote.

1.1 What to Footnote

All Primary and Secondary resources, such as case-law, legislations, books, journals, reports, etc. that one uses to augment an argument or to provide information, should be created as a footnote. However, the author should be cautious from 'over-documenting' the research and should omit the use of irrelevant sources or many sources providing the same information. 'Over documentation' distracts the reader from the main text. At the same time, 'under-documenting' the research risks the reliability and veracity of the claim being made by the author. In other words, it is not correct to believe that a stronger research paper is founded upon a great volume of references. A good research paper can well be written by referring to a few, yet good and meaningful resources.

1.2 Why to Footnote

It is imperative to footnote the source when we borrow somebody's idea to support our argument or when we borrow somebody's research to develop our argument or when we borrow somebody's statistics for descriptive or analytical papers. Creating footnotes serves the purpose of preventing plagiarism by acknowledging the research conducted by others in subject area thereby protecting the intellectual property rights of authors and publishers, and helps researchers working in the same subject area to identify and locate the source.

1.3 When to Footnote

Footnotes should be created under the following circumstances: (1) at the first reference to the source, (2) at every subsequent quotation from the source, (3) at every subsequent allusion or reference to a particular passage to a source. The full citation must be provided in the first footnote referring to a source.

1.4 Content Footnote

In addition to the reference to the citation of a particular source, footnotes can sometimes be used to provide additional information to the reader or comments that you do not want to include in the main body of the paper. It is a useful way of providing additional information without breaking the flow of the argument in the paper.

1.5 How to indicate a Footnote in the Text

In legal writing, footnotes are indicated by numbers, and not by Roman numerals or special characters. Use of Control, Alt. and F Keys together is probably the easiest way to insert a footnote while writing your main text. As a matter of practice, the footnotes are placed at the end of a paraphrased sentence or at the end of the borrowed quotation after the punctuation mark.[1] When referring to a particular word or term coined by another author, place the footnote number directly after the word. When quoting from a source, place the footnote after the ending of the "quotation marks" and/or "the punctuation".[2]

1.6 Where Footnotes appear

Footnotes, unlike endnotes, usually appear at the bottom of the same page where the author refers to the arguments of other authors in the text. In rare circumstances, when the footnotes are too long, they may stretch to the next page, at the most.

1.7 Footnotes to end with a period

A full stop should generally appear at the end of every footnote.

1.8 When to combine Footnotes

Various sources/references that support an argument can be combined into one footnote. In such a case, the citations to two or more sources in a footnote should be separated by a semi-colon (;) and the entire footnote must end with a period (.). Where quoting from a particular source and other sources support the same argument, the source from where the quotation is being borrowed should be cited first in the footnote and other references/sources should follow. *E.g.*:—

> Bruce MacDougall, *Queer Judgments: Homosexuality, Expression and the Courts in Canada* (Toronto: University of Toronto Press, 2000) at 236; Ty S. Twibell, "Immigrant Nations: A Comparison of the Immigration Law of Australia and the United States" (2000) 19 U. Tas. L. Rev. 57 at 78.

1.9 Introductory signals in Footnotes

An introductory signal is sometimes used to explain the purpose or logical relationship between the source cited and the proposition in the text. In other words, introductory signals are used to present authorities and show how the authorities relate to propositions in textual statements. It is used to inform the readers how the legal authority supports, or does not support, the written proposition. Introductory signals help organize the writer's citations into a hierarchy of strength and importance so that the reader can quickly determine the relative weight of each citation. Introductory signals should not be italicised except where required by Universal's Guide to Uniform Legal Citations. The first letter of a signal should be capitalized when it begins a citation sentence. However, if the signal appears within a citation sentence, *i.e.* after a semicolon (;), it should not be capitalized. Further, a single space should separate an introductory signal from the rest of the citation, with no punctuation, like a period, comma or semicolon, in between. No indicator should be used where the authority is quoted directly or directly states the proposition made in the text. The following table presents some introductory signals and the purpose for which they are used:

See	When the authority cited clearly supports but does not directly state the proposition given in the text. If the authority clearly and directly states and supports the proposition, we do not use any indicator. It can be used to establish inferential relationship between the authority cited and the proposition given in the text to show that the proposition flows directly from the cited authority. It may also be used to refer to a cited authority that contains dicta in support of the proposition being made.

See especially	When the authority cited is the strongest of several that support the proposition given in the text.
See *e.g.*	It literally means, "for example". When the authority cited is one of the several that support the proposition given in the text, but the other supporting authorities are not cited.
See generally	When the authority cited supports and provides background information to the proposition in the text. When using 'see generally' it is advisable that the authors provide the brief relevance of the source in parenthesis ( ).
See also	When the authority cited provides added/ qualified/general support to the proposition in the text, but is not the most authoritative source or is tangent on the point. It generally follows a direct source on the subject and is not as authoritative as the source cited first. When using 'see also' it is advisable that the authors provide the brief relevance of the source in parenthesis ( ).
Accord	When the authority cited provides added direct support to the proposition in the text, and is as authoritative as the source cited first. It is generally used when two or more sources state or support the proposition, and the text already quotes or refers to one of them; the other sources are then introduced by "accord." Accord is also used to show that the law of one jurisdiction is in accord with that of another jurisdiction.
Cf.	When the authority cited supports a different, but analogous proposition to lend support to the current proposition. It is used when the cited authority does not exactly support the proposition, but it's close enough to lend support. When using '*Cf.*' it is advisable that the authors provide the brief relevance of the source in parenthesis ( ).
Compare	When the authority cited provides a useful contrast to illustrate the current proposition.
But see	When the authority cited provides partial disagreement with the proposition stated in the text, but does not directly contradict it. This indicator is usually used when discussing the merits of a particular

	proposition. It usually follows the authorities that directly support the proposition in the text to present the other side of the coin.
But cf.	When the cited authority contradicts the given proposition by way of analogy. When using *'But cf.'* it is advisable that the authors provide the brief relevance of the source in parenthesis ( ).
Contra	When the authority cited directly contradicts the proposition in the text.
Compare _____with_____ **Compare _____and____with____** **Compare___and___with___and___** ***Compare__with___and___***	When the author wishes to compare two or more authorities that reach different outcomes to the given proposition. Both *compare* and *with* may be followed by more than one source, using an italicised *and* between them. *Compare, with* and *and* should be italicised, while the authorities should be stated in non-italics. As the relevance of the comparison may not be readily apparent to the reader, it is advisable that the authors provide the brief relevance of the source in parenthesis ( ).

1.9.1 What to include in Parenthesis

Explanatory information in parenthesis is a short statement explaining the relevance of the source. If quoting the short statement from the authority, the first alphabet of the statement in parenthesis should begin with a capital letter. If not quoting the short statement from the authority, the first alphabet of the statement in parenthesis should never begin with a capital letter.

1.9.2 Order of introductory signals

Organizing the order of introductory signals in long footnotes helps the reader identify the strength of the authorities cited. When multiple introductory signals occur in one footnote, the order of signals should be as follows: No signal, accord, see, see especially, see *e.g.*, see also, *cf.*, compare, *compare___with___, contra,* but see, *but cf.*, see generally. As a rule, one must start with the strongest, most direct support, then analogous, then negative and then general.

1.10 Order of authorities within a Footnote

When combining various references/sources that support an argument, as a rule, strongest authorities, then direct, then analogous, then negative and then general should be cited. If there are many authorities in each category or within each introductory signal, primary authorities should be cited first and then the secondary authorities should follow. Primary and secondary sources can be further ordered as follows:

Primary Sources

1.10.1 Constitutional and other foundational documents:

i. Federal
ii. State (alphabetical order)
iii. Foreign (alphabetical order by jurisdiction)
iv. Foundational documents for United Nations
v. Foundational documents for League of Nations
vi. Foundational documents for the European Union

1.10.2 Statutes/Legislations

i. Federal or Central statutes
ii. State statutes (alphabetical order)
iii. Foreign statutes (alphabetical order by jurisdiction)

1.10.3 Treaties and other International Agreements

i. Treaties entered into by parties to UN
ii. Multinational treaties
iii. Bi-national treaties

1.10.4 Case-law

i. **Supreme Court**
   - Full Bench
   - Constitutional Bench (comprising of 5 or more Judges). Within this category the cases with highest Bench strength should be cited first, *e.g.* 13 Judges, 11 Judges, 9 Judges, 7 judges, 5 judges.
   - Reference, larger Bench (when referred to the larger Bench by Division Bench of Supreme Court)
   - Division Bench (comprising 2 Judges)
   - Reference, Division Bench
   - Reference, Single Bench
   - Appeals, writs and Public Interest Litigations, etc.

ii. **Privy Council**
iii. **Federal Court**
iv. **Other Courts**
   - Lahore Court
   - Nagpur
   - Oudh
   - Peshawar

- Rangoon
- Sind

v. **High Court (Alphabetical order)**
- Full Bench
- Division Bench
- Single Bench

vi. **District Criminal Courts** (Alphabetical order)
- District and Additional District Judge
- Additional Sessions Judge
- ACMM
- Metropolitan Magistrates

vii. **District Civil Courts** (Alphabetical order)
- District and Additional District Judge
- Additional Sessions Judge
- Courts of Rent Controllers and Civil Judges
- Courts of CMM/ACMM/MM
- Court of Special Judges
- Court of Children Courts

viii. **Other Tribunals in the District Courts' Complex** (Alphabetical Order)
- Appellate Tribunal for MCD and NDMC
- Industrial Tribunals
- Labour Courts
- Motor Accidents Claims Tribunal
- Traffic Courts

ix. **Other Administrative Tribunals or Courts outside the District Courts' Complex** (Alphabetical Order)
- Central Administrative Tribunals
- State Administrative Tribunals
- Other Appellate Tribunals (alphabetical order), such as Appellate Tribunal for Electricity, Central Excise Service Tax Appellate Tribunal, Debt Recovery Appellate Tribunal, Income Tax Appellate Tribunal, Intellectual Property Appellate Tribunal,
- Other tribunals (alphabetical order) such as Debt Recovery Tribunal, Railway Claims Tribunals, etc.
- Other appellate courts (alphabetical order) such as First Appeals, Consumer Courts or Revision Petition, Consumer Courts, etc.

- Other courts (alphabetical order) such as Consumer Courts, Company Law Boards, etc.

x. **Foreign Courts** (alphabetical order by jurisdiction)
- Federal/Supreme Courts
- Appellate Courts
- District Courts

xi. **International**
- International Court of Justice
- Permanent Court of International Justice
- International Criminal Court
- International Criminal Tribunal for Rwanda
- International Criminal Tribunal for Yugoslavia
- Other International Tribunals (alphabetical order)

1.10.5 Arbitration

i. Domestic Arbitration
ii. Foreign Arbitration
iii. International Arbitration

1.10.6 Other Legislative Materials (Domestic, Foreign and International)

i. Bills and resolutions
ii. Committee hearings
iii. Reports (Law Commission and others)
iv. Documents
v. Floor debates or minutes

Secondary Sources

i. Books (single author and multiple author)
ii. Books (essay collections)
iii. Articles in Peer Reviewed journals
iv. Articles in Student Reviewed journals
v. Book reviews by Professionals
vi. Book reviews by Students
vii. Pamphlets
viii. Magazines
ix. News paper articles
x. Working papers
xi. Unpublished materials
xii. Electronic sources

1.11 Internal Cross References

Cross references to points of important discussions perform the useful function of directing the reader to the relevant part of your paper/thesis where you have presented similar or supporting arguments. However, one should avoid directing the reader to another part of the text if a short note or statement in the footnote could have served the purpose. In any case, a single source may be referred to many times in a single text. The full citation should be indicated in the footnote accompanying the first reference to the source. The author should create short titles for subsequent references. Short title can be created in the following ways:

Primary Sources

1. **CASES:** A short title can be created by choosing one of the party's names/surnames. It is advisable that where State or Union of India is one of the parties, the author should choose the name/title of the other party for reference. *E.g. Kesavananda Bharti* v. *State of Kerela,* AIR 1973 SC 1461 can be referred to as *Kesavananda Bharti* for subsequent reference. Similarly, *Shankari Prasad* v. *Union of India,* AIR 1951 SC 458 can be written as *Shankari Prasad,* for subsequent reference. As a matter of general practice, it is advisable to use the name of the first party, *i.e.* the applicant, appellant, revisionist, petitioner, etc., except where State is the first party.

2. **LEGISLATIONS:** Where a statute provides for a short title, the same should be used for subsequent reference. Where the original title of the legislation is brief, there is no need to create a short title. *E.g.* **Indian Contract Act, 1872** can be subsequently referred to as **Indian Contract Act** omitting the year in which it came into force. If there is no official short title, it is advisable that the author should create a distinctive and meaningful short title. *E.g.* **Prevention of Domestic Violence Against Women Act, 2005** can be written as **Domestic Violence Act** for subsequent reference. Similarly **Muslim Women (Protection of Rights on Divorce) Act, 1986** can be referred to as **Muslim Women Divorce Rights Act.**

The author may also choose to create an abbreviation for the legislation if the original title is too long although it is advisable that the author refrain from this practice. If the author chooses to follow the abbreviation style for legislations, he/she must ensure that he/she follows the abbreviation style for legislations throughout his/her work/paper/research/article to maintain consistency and clarity. It is advisable that the author creates a list of abbreviations to be appended to his/her work to help the reader clearly identify the legislation at one place instead of looking for relevant footnotes back and forth. *E.g. The Cable Television Networks (Regulation) Ordinance Act, 1995* can be subsequently referred to as *CTNRO*. However, it is important that the author so abbreviating should state the abbreviation within [ ] at the time of making first reference to the source. *E.g.*

1 The Cable Television Networks (Regulation) Ordinance Act, 1995, section 5 [CTNRO].

2 The Cinematograph Act, 1952, section 10.

3 CTNRO, *supra* note 1.

Secondary Sources

A short title can be created by using the author's surname to make subsequent reference to the source. *E.g.* Upendra Baxi, *Human Rights in a Post-Human World: Critical Essays* (India: Oxford University Press, 2007) at 76 can be referred to as Baxi, *supra note # at page number*. If more than one work by a particular author is being cited, the author should create a short title comprising of the surname of the author and a short form of the title of the work. The short title so created should be placed within brackets at the time of making the first reference to the source. *E.g.*

1. Upendra Baxi, *Human Rights in a Post-Human World: Critical Essays* (India: Oxford University Press, 2007) at 76 [Baxi, *Critical Essays*].
2. R.N. Trivedi, *World of All Human Rights, Soli J. Sorabjee – A Festschrift* (India: Universal Law Publishing Co. Pvt. Ltd., 2010) at 50.
3. Upendra Baxi, *The Future of Human Rights* (India: Oxford University Press, 2002) at 42 [Baxi, *The Future*].
4. Asia Watch, *Human Rights in the APEC Region* (New York: Asia Watch, 1993) at 30.
5. Baxi, *Critical Essays, supra* note 1 at 80.
6. Asia Watch, *supra* note 4 at 31.
7. Baxi, *The Future, supra* note 3 at 45.
8. Justice J.S. Verma, *The New Universe of Human Rights* (India: Universal Law Publishing Co. Pvt. Ltd., 2006) at 50.

In the short form for title, maintain the same formating as the full title, *i.e.* italics for books and quotation marks for the articles.

References to the full citation in the footnotes can be done in the following ways:

Supra	Supra is a latin word meaning "above". It is used to refer the reader to a previous footnote containing complete citation to the source being referred to. It should refer the reader to the original and complete citation and not to another *supra* or *ibid*. *Supra* can, however, be combined with introductory signals like see, *Cf.*, see especially, etc. To refer to a previous footnote for citation, use *supra* note #, at page number. *Supra* should be italicized while the remaining

	footnote should be non-italics. The clause *supra* note #(,) ends with comma if accompanied by a page number or else it ends with a period. *e.g.* author's last name, *supra* note 5, at page number. If the author wishes to refer the reader to the original citation as well as accompanying text, use *supra* note # and accompanying text. *e.g.* See also author's last name, *supra* note 15 and accompanying text. The author should create a short form/title of the original source, which can be used while referring to it subsequently. *E.g.* 1. *Kesavananda Bharti* v. *State of Kerela,* AIR 1973 SC 1461 (1467) [Kesavananda Bharti]. 2. *Shankari Prasad* v. *Union of India,* AIR 1951 SC 458 (459) [Shankari Prasad]. 3. *Kesavananda Bharti, supra* note 1 at 1468. 4. *Golak Nath* v. *State of Punjab,* (1967) 2 SCR 762 (767). 5. *Shankari Prasad, supra* note 2 and accompanying text.
Infra	*Infra* is a latin term meaning 'below'. Use infra to refer to a subsequent footnote. As with *supra, infra* can be combined with introductory signals. Use of *infra* should be usually avoided. To refer to a previous footnote for citation, use *infra* note # at page number. *Infra* should be italicized while the remaining footnote should be non italics. The clause *infra* note # at # ends with a period. *e.g.* author's last name, *infra* note 5 at page number. The author should create a short form/title of the original source, which can be used while referring to it. *E.g.* 1. Baxi, *Critical Essays, infra* note 5 at 80. 2. R.N. Trivedi, *World of All Human Rights, Soli Sorabjee – A Festschrift* (India: Universal Law Publishing Co. Pvt. Ltd., 2010) at 50. 3. Upendra Baxi, *The Future of Human Rights* (India: Oxford University Press, 2002) at 42 [Baxi, *The Future*].

	4. Asia Watch, *Human Rights in the APEC Region* (New York: Asia Watch, 1993) at 30. 5. Upendra Baxi, *Human Rights in a Post-Human World: Critical Essays* (India: Oxford University Press, 2007) at 76 [Baxi, *Critical Essays*]. 6. Asia Watch, *supra* note 4 at 31. 7. Baxi, *The Future, supra* note 3 at 45 8. Justice D.M. Dharmadhikari, *Human Values and Human Rights* (India: Universal Law Publishing Co. Pvt. Ltd., 2010) at 81.
Ibid.	*Ibid.* is an abbreviation of the Latin word *ibidem,* meaning "in the same place". It is used to direct the reader to the immediately preceding reference without providing the number of the footnote being referred to. *Ibid.* may be used after a complete citation, after a *supra* or even after another *ibid.* A short title only needs to be created if there is more than one source in the preceding footnote. *Ibid.* means strictly 'in the very same place' while *ibid.* with a different page number signifies 'in the same work but at a different page'. Thus, if *ibid.* is being used without pin-pointing the page number, it is taken to mean that the author is referring to the same page number stated in the preceding source. *Examples:* 1. *Kesavananda Bharti* v. *State of Kerela,* AIR 1973 SC 1461 at 1467 [Kesavananda Bharti], *Shankari Prasad* v. *Union of India,* AIR 1951 SC 458 at 459 [Shankari Prasad]. 2. Kesavananda Bharti, *ibid.* at 1465. 3. *Golak Nath* v. *State of Punjab,* (1967) 2 SCR 762 at 767. 4. *Ibid.* 5. Shankari Prasad, *supra* note 1 at 461. 6. *Ibid. at 463.*

'Above' and 'Below' can be used to direct a reader to a particular portion of the text, and not *supra* and *infra* as the latter are meant for directing a reader to prior or subsequent footnotes. It is advisable to only direct the reader to the portions of the text if the text is structured and divided in identifiable parts, sections or marked paragraphs. If the text is not structured or divided into identifiable parts, sections or paragraphs, the use of 'above' and 'below' should be avoided. In such a situation, the author could use "*supra* note # and accompanying text."

Above	Above is used to direct the reader to a portion of the text already discussed to avoid repetition and to link the current sub-argument with another sub-argument or main argument. 1. R.N. Trivedi, *World of All Human Rights, Soli Sorabjee – A Festschrift* (India: Universal Law Publishing Co. Pvt. Ltd., 2010) at 50. 2. P.H. Parekh, *Human Rights Year Book* (India: Universal Law Publishing Co. Pvt. Ltd., 2010) at 50. 3. See Part II.B, above, for the argument on universality of Human Rights.
Below	Below is used to direct the reader to the portion of the text that the author wishes to discuss later. 1. Asia Watch, *Human Rights in the APEC Region* (New York: Asia Watch, 1993) at 30. 2. Further discussion on the infringement of Human Rights in Third World countries will be found in Part IVA, at 60-63, below. 3. Upendra Baxi, *Human Rights in a Post-Human World: Critical Essays* (India: Oxford University Press, 2007) at 76 [Baxi, *Critical Essays*].

The author should not use other obsolete terms for cross reference, like op. cit. and *loc. cit.*

1.12 Citing Sources that Quote an Original Source

It is advisable to always refer to the original source, if available. Every effort must be made to find the original source and verify the information therein. However, if for some reason, the author is unable to locate and verify the source and information, he/she should provide the complete citation and use 'cited in' to refer both to the current source and to the original source he/she found relevant in the current source. Using 'cited in' cautions the reader that he/she is reading unverified information and it is not safe to rely upon the same for the purpose of his/her research. The author can refer to the original source in the current source in the following way:

[First Name][Last Name] of the Author of Original source, *Name of the Book* (Place of Publication: Name of Publishers, Year of Publication) at page number, cited in [First Name][Last Name] of the Author of Current source, *Name of the Book* (Place of Publication: Name of Publishers, Year of Publication) at page number.

The author can likewise refer to the original source stated in journal articles or reports by following the respective citation formats that are explained later.

1.13 In-text Citations: Rules

In Legal Factums and Memorandums, the authors may add the citations directly in the text instead of using footnotes. Sources should be cited at the end of the relevant sentence within parenthesis. If citing a source subsequently, a short form should be created within brackets after the end of parenthesis, *e.g.* (*Hussainara Khatoon* v. *State of Bihar*, AIR 1979 SC 1360: (1980) 1 SCC 81) [Hussainara Khatoon]. Full and complete citation to the source should be included in the bibliography at the end of the factum/memorandum. The initials of authors should not be given, except where reference is made to more than one author with the same last name. Subsequent in-text citations should follow the following format:

The author's last name, the year in which the work was published and the relevant page number(s) or figure or table number must be given in brackets: (Lloyd 1980, 142).

When writing an essay, there is no need to cite complete reference of the source in text. A short reference within parenthesis at the end of the sentence comprising of last name of the author, year of publication and page number should serve the purpose in case of books/articles *e.g.* (Hart 1980, 56). In case of legislations, abbreviated title should serve the purpose *e.g.* (Domestic Violence Act, 2005). In case of jurisprudence/case-law, the name of any of the parties could be used *e.g.* (Shankari Prasad). Full and complete reference to each of the sources should be given in endnotes.

> From an illegal and impermissible 'union' of 'undesirable aliens', same sex relationships have come a long way, to be recognized as 'family', not only in the edifice of the family law but also in other areas of law, such as immigration, tax and property etc. The notions of marriage and family, which were once considered essentially a union of man and a woman along with other attributes of companionship and mutual support, have expanded to recognize the rights of same sex couples. (*Corbett* v. *Corbett*)
>
> The history is a witness to the discrimination faced by the gays and lesbians in their struggle for equal rights. Half a century ago, some of the esteemed western nations considered homosexuals as individuals with a 'psychopathic constitutional inferiority'. (Scaperlanda 2003, 216; United States, 1917 Act)

The United States of America barred the entry of gays and lesbians as 'persons of abnormal sexual instincts.' (Scaperlanda 2003, 217)

1.13.1 *Dual or Multiple References*

For dual or multiple references in a single sentence, references should be listed in alphabetical order separated by a semi colon. *E.g.* (Bailey 1981; Jones 1970; Peters 1997)

1.13.2 *Reference to Book or Articles by multiple authors*

When an article or book has two authors, both must be cited using '&' between the last names of the authors *e.g.* (Bailey & Smith, 1996). When an article or book has more than two authors, the last name of first author is used followed by italicised *et al.* and the date of publication *e.g.* (Smith *et al.*, 1980).

1.13.3 *Reference to different works of the same author in a given year*

When referring to different works of the same author in a given year, they should be cited by abbreviating the titles of articles or books *e.g.* Last name of the author, abbreviated title, year of publication.

E.g. (Baxi, Mambrino's Helmet, 1994; Baxi, Inhuman Wrongs, 1994)

1.13.4 *Reference to a work whose author is unknown*

In the absence of the name/surname of the author, the name of the publishers should be used followed by the abbreviated title of the work and year of publication, (Universal Law Publishing Co. Pvt. Ltd., *Rights of Accused*, 2009).

1.13.5 *Reference to the original source cited in another source*

If referring to an original source cited in the current source, both should be stated in the text *e.g.* (Bailey, 1975 cited in Smith, 1980).

1.14 Quotations: Rules

Quotations are usually extracts verbatim lifted from another author's work to be incorporated in one's work. If another's idea is being stated verbatim, it should ideally be marked in such a way that a reader can distinguish your work from that of another. It is also imperative that you pin-point the exact page number of the source from where the passage is lifted.

1.14.1 *Short and Long Quotations*

In the text-body and footnotes, short quotations (of four lines or less) should be incorporated in the text within double quotation marks (" ").

E.g.

I hypothesize that the degree of responsibility is determined by stressing upon the actions of the offender or her state of mind. While considering the degree of responsibility of the offender, the scope of limiting the punishment exists if the offender suffered from a state of diminished responsibility owing to insanity or any other psychiatric condition or intoxication. The absence of a psychiatric condition is used to justify the punishment. In the cases that I reviewed, there were little discussions about the "degree of responsibility". In *Ferguson* case, it was rightly observed that the "[d]egree of responsibility does not only refer to the participation of the offender and the offence committed, it refers to a legal measure of guilt considering all of the circumstances leading to the commission of the offence, and when and how the offence was actually committed."

Long quotations (more than four lines) should be indented from both margins, single spaced, be one font size smaller than rest of the text and without quotation marks. Legislative provisions, even though less than four lines, may be indented in a similar way.

E.g. The accused's past abuse and her successful attempts at overcoming her substance abuse were mitigating factors, but they did not justify a sentence below the normal range. The court of appeal warned the sentencing judges that:

> [A] sentencing judge should be cautious about placing too much emphasis on reformation which has taken place by reference only to a period following the laying of charges, and the imposition of sentence. Sentences should fit crimes and generally speaking the need for treatment for a physical or mental disorder should not be considered in imposing sentence.

1.14.2 Whether any changes to original quotation are permitted

As a matter of rule, there should be no changes in the spelling, grammar, capitalization and internal punctuation in a quote, even if you think that the author should have done so to simplify the sentence or if that would grammatically correct the sentence. The quotation must be exactly the same as in the original source. Any changes or rectification of errors should be introduced in brackets [ ].

Where a full stop (.) or a colon (:) precedes a quotation, the first letter of the quotation should be capitalized within [ ] if the original quotation does not begin with capital letter. If the original quotation begins with a capital letter, the author need not introduce brackets as he/she is not making any changes to the original quotation.

Similarly, where comma (,) or semi-colon (;) precedes a quotation, or the quotation becomes the part of a sentence, and the original quotation begins with a capital letter, the first alphabet should be changed to lower case within brackets.

1.14.3 Introducing Ellipsis

An ellipsis (...) is used to indicate the omission of a part of the passage/paragraph, whether from the beginning, middle or end.

E.g.	In *Kahypeasewat* case, the Hon'ble Court relying upon the *Proulx* case observed that: The Supreme Court of Canada made it clear in *Proulx* that severe restrictions on the offender's liberty are to be the norm and not the exception...A person who serves the sentence in the community still carries a societal stigma...[D]eterrence, to the extent that it is effective, can be satisfied by the imposition of a community-based sentence.

1.14.4 Change of Emphasis

Any change of emphasis from the original, *i.e.* change of font size or style, should be indicated in parenthesis after citation as (emphasis added). If there is no change in emphasis from the original, and the original text used italicised or used bold to emphasize the text, (emphasis in original) should be added after the quotation.

1.14.5 Omissions of Citations

If the footnotes of the original text are omitted, place (footnotes omitted) at the end of the citation.

1.15 Bibliographies: Rules

A Bibliography should state all the primary and secondary resources relied upon by the author.

1.15.1 Division in Sections

A legal bibliography should be divided into the following sections in the given order:

1.15.1.1 Primary Resources

i. Legislations

ii. Case-Law

iii. Other Government Materials

iv. Treaties

1.15.1.2 Secondary Resources

i. Books

ii. Articles, Notes and Comments

iii. Newspaper Reports/Articles

iv. Papers presented at conferences/seminars/lectures

v. Dictionaries

vi. Electronic Resources

vii. Other Secondary resources

1.15.2 *Alphabetical Order*

Each entry within the sub-sections should be in alphabetical order.

1.15.3 *Format of Bibliography*

While bibliographical citation of legislation, jurisprudence, government materials and treaties should follow the rules indicated in Universal's Guide to Uniform Legal Citations, references to secondary materials are cited differently in the context of a bibliography or list of authorities, than when used in footnotes. For secondary material, the author's family name appears first.

1.15.4 *Two or more than two authors*

Where two authors have authored/edited a book or an article, their last names are combined together with "&" between their names, *e.g.* Smith, Hugh & Williams, Peter.

Where more than two authors have authored/edited a book or an article, their names are abbreviated by *et al.* and only the name of the first author/editor of the collection is given, *e.g.* Williams, Peter *et al.*

1.15.5 *Two authors sharing the same name*

Where two authors share the same family name, the order of bibliography is determined according to the alphabetical order of their first names.

Following is an example of a Bibliography containing primary and secondary sources:

LEGISLATION

1. *The Code of Criminal Procedure,* 1973.
2. *The Constitution of India,* 1950.
3. *The Gram Nyayalayas Bill,* 2007, Bill No. XXXVII of 2007.
4. *The Indian Penal Code,* 45 of 1860.
5. *The Protection of Women from Domestic Violence Act,* 2005.

JURISPRUDENCE

1. *B.S. Joshi* v. *State of Haryana,* AIR 2003 SC 1386.
2. *Basara* v. *State,* (3rd September, 2007) Delhi Crl. M.C. No. 6621-24/2006 (Delhi High Court).
3. *Hussainara Khatoon* v. *State of Bihar,* (1980) 1 SCC 81: AIR 1979 SC 1360.

GOVERNMENT MATERIALS

Government of India, "Alternative Dispute Resolution" (Paper presented by the Government of India in the meeting of Common Law Ministers, New Zealand) (1990) May-August Legal Aid News Letter.

TREATIES

Convention *on the Rights of Child,* opened for signature 20th November, 1989, 1588 UNTS 530 (entered into force 16th January, 1991).

SECONDARY MATERIALS: MONOGRAPHS

1. Hosbet, Suresh *All Human Rights are Fundamental Rights* (India: Universal Law Publishing Co. Pvt. Ltd., 2010).
2. Beals, Alan R. *Village India; studies in the little community* (Chicago: University of Chicago Press, 1967).
3. Becker, Howard S. *Outsiders: Studies in the Sociology of Deviance* (London, Free Press of Glencoe [c1963]; London: Collier-Macmillan, 1973).

SECONDARY MATERIALS: ARTICLES, NOTES AND COMMENTS

Aggarwal, Manu. & Kaura, Meera. "Mediation in Penal Law" (2005-2006) II DLR 15.

SECONDARY MATERIALS: NEWSPAPER REPORTS/ARTICLES

Bhushan, Shanti. "Will to Change Needed", *Onlooker* (15th July, 1990).

SECONDARY MATERIALS: PAPERS PRESENTED AT CONFERENCES/ LECTURES/SEMINARS

Galanter, Marc. & Krishnan, Jayanth. "Debased Informalism: Lok Adalats and Legal Rights in Modern India" (Paper presented at the First South Asian Regional Judicial Colloquium on Access to Justice at New Delhi, 1-3 November, 2002).

SECONDARY MATERIALS: MISCELLANEOUS

Sylvestre, Marie-Eve *Policing Disorder and Criminalizing the Homeless in Montreal and Rio de Janeiro: A critique of the Justifications for Repression in Law and Practice,* (Thesis, Harvard Law School, 2007) [unpublished].

SECONDARY MATERIALS: DICTIONARIES

The American Heritage Dictionary of the English Language, 4th Edn., 2002.

1.16 Endnotes: Rules

Use of endnotes should be avoided in legal writing, except where authors are writing essays, notes and comments.

1.16.1 *What to Endnote*

All Primary and Secondary resources, such as, case-law, legislations, books, journals and reports, etc., that you use to present your views, should be created as endnotes.

1.16.2 *Why to Endnote*

It is imperative to endnote to acknowledge the source of our idea or contention.

1.16.3 *How to indicate an Endnote in the Text*

In legal writing, endnotes are indicated by numbers, and not by Roman numerals or special characters. Endnotes can be easily created by choosing References Tab in Microsoft Word, 2007. Locate the footnote section and then open Footnote and Endnote Dialog Box. Select Endnote in the Footnote and Endnote Dialog Box. Display the "Number format" drop-down list, and then choose the type of numbering format. Click on"Apply" button to apply the changes and close the Footnote and Endnote Dialog box.

1.16.4 *Where Endnotes appear*

Endnotes appear at the end of the document.

1.16.5 *Endnotes to end with a period*

A full stop should generally appear at the end of every endnote.

1.16.6 *When to combine Endnotes*

Various sources/references that support an argument can be combined into one endnote. In such a case, the citations to two or more sources in an endnote should be separated by a semi-colon (;) and the entire endnote must end with a period (.).

1.16.7 *Introductory Signals and Cross-references*

All introductory signals stated in footnote section can be used in endnotes. *Supra* and *Ibid* can be used in endnotes.

1.16.8 *Format of Endnotes*

The endnotes are inserted at the end of the relevant sentences and hence appear in a chronological order. The endnotes follow the same format for all primary and secondary resources as footnotes, except in the case of secondary resources, where author's last name appears first. The following is an example of endnotes accompanying an essay:

1. Dhir, Aaron A. "Same-Sex Family Class Immigration: Is the Definition of Spouse in Canada's Immigration Regulations, 1978 Unconstitutional" (2000) 49 New Brunswick Law Journal 183 at 196.
2. *Immigration Act*, R.S.C. 1952, c. 325, sections 5 and 19(1)(e).
3. *Corbett* v. *Corbett (Ashley)*, (No. 2), [1970] 2 All ER 22 (48).

4. *See* Ryder, Bruce. "Equality Rights and Sexual Orientation: Confronting Heterosexual Family Privilege", (1990) 9 Can. J. Fam. L. 39 at 49-62 and 89-97; Casswell, Donald G. *Lesbians, Gay Men, and the Canadian Law* (Toronto: E. Montgomery Publications, 1996) at 564; Lahey, Kathleen A. *Are we Persons Yet? Law and Sexuality in Canada* (Toronto; Buffalo: University of Toronto Press, 1999) at 138; LaViolette, Nicole. "Coming Out to Canada: The Immigration of Same Sex Couples under Immigration and Refugee Protection Act" (2004) 49 McGill L.J. 969 at 973; *Dhir, supra* note 1 at 186, 187.
5. Paulson, Joanne. "Gay People deserve equal treatment under immigration law: activists" *Star Phoenix*, Monday (24th November, 1997) A6; Casswell, Donald G. "Same Sex Partners and Family Class Immigration: Still not Equal with Opposite Sex Partners" (Spring 2004) 27 Dalhousie LJ 203.
6. Homophobia refers to "a feeling of fear expressed towards homosexuals and more generally persons whose appearance or conduct departs from the norms of virility. Contempt, disgust, prejudice and hatred targeting homosexuals grow out of this fear. Homophobia is to some extent an aggressive reaction of rejection caused by this fear of emotional relations between men or between women, whether they are sexual or not". This definition has been taken from Demczuk, Irene *et al.*, *Recognition of Lesbian Couples: An Inalienable Right* (Ottawa, Canada: Status of Women Canada, 2002).

2
LEGISLATION

INDIA

2.1 Statutes

2.1.1 General Form: Central Statutes

Official Short Title of the Act/Code,	Act Title and/or Object of the Act,	Pinpoint the section.
The Protection of Women from Domestic Violence Act,	No. 43 of 2005,	s. 18.
Foreign Marriage Act	Act No. 33 of 1969,	s. 12.
The Copyright Act,	Act No. 14 of 1957, An Act to Amend and Consolidate the Law Relating to Copyright,	s. 54.
The Foreign Trade (Development and Regulation) Act,	Act No. 22 of 1992,	s. 14.
Indian Penal Code,	Act No. 45 of 1860,	s. 300.

- Italicize the official short title (excluding the year) of the statute and place a non-italicized comma after the short title.
- The official short title of the statute, usually provided in chapter 1, section 1 or 2 of every statute, should be compulsorily provided when making the first reference to the statute.
- If a statute does not provide an official short title, the title found at the head of the statute should be provided when making the first reference to the statute. Use "The" only if it forms the part of the title.
- If the short title is brief, it may also be used in subsequent references (*e.g.* the *Copyright Act*).
- If a statute has no official short title, or if the official short title is too long for subsequent references, a distinctive short title should be created and indicated in brackets at the end of the citation.

- The Act title can be usually found in chapter 1, section 1 of every statute. If a private publisher has not provided the Act title of a central statute, indiacode.nic.in provides all authentic central statutes online. Use "Act" only if a statute provides for the same in the title. *E.g.* the Act title of *The Protection of Women from Domestic Violence Act* begins as No. 43 of 2005 and not Act No. 43 of 2005.
- If a statute does not provide an Act title, simply state the official short title in italics followed by a non-italicized comma and a non-italicized year, *e.g.* *Protection of Women from Domestic Violence Act*, 2005.

2.1.2 *General Form: State Statutes*

Official Short Title,	Name of the State,	Year,	Pinpoint
The Kerela Finance Act,		2005,	s. 10.
Andhra Pradesh Water, Land and Trees Act,		2002,	s. 14.
Gujarat Control of Organized Crimes Act,		2003,	s. 10
The Slum Rehabilitation Act,	Maharashtra,	1995,	s. 12.
West Bengal Societies Registration Act,		1961,	s. 2.
Gudalur Janmam Estates (Abolition and Conversion into Ryotwari) Act,	Tamil Nadu,	1969,	s. 3.

- Italicize the official short title (excluding the year) of the statute and place a non-italicized comma after the short title.
- The official short title of the statute, usually provided in chapter 1, section 1 or 2 of every statute, should be compulsorily provided when making the first reference to the statute.
- If a statute does not provide an official short title, the title found at the head of the statute should be provided when making the first reference to the statute. Use "The" only if it forms the part of the title.
- If the short title is brief, it may also be used in subsequent references (*e.g.* the *Kerela Finance Act*).
- If a statute has no official short title, or if the official short title is too long for subsequent references, a distinctive short title should be created and indicated in brackets at the end of the citation.
- It is not necessary to provide for the Act title of State Legislations.
- Provide for the name of the State only if the official short title of the statute does not provide the same. *E.g.* Maharashtra does not

precede the official short title of *The Slum Rehabilitation Act.* Here it is necessary to provide the name of the State (jurisdiction) after the short title. There is no need to provide the name of the State separately where the name of the State precedes the official short title or is included in the official short title.

2.1.3 *Pinpoints*

- To refer to a specific section of a statute, comma should be placed after the Act title and then indicate the section. If referring to only one section, use "s." to indicate section followed by the section number. If referring to multiple sections, use "ss." to indicate sections followed by the section numbers, *e.g.* ss. 9, 14 or ss. 10-17. If referring to particular numbered sub-section or paragraph of a section, there is no need to abbreviate the sub-section. The sub-section/paragraph number can follow the main section in parenthesis. *E.g.* s. 9(1)(iv). If referring to multiple sub-sections of a section(s), separate them by comma, *e.g.* s. 9(1)(iii), 9(1)(iv), 9(1)(v) or ss. 9(1)(iii), 10(2)(ii), 14(1)(vi). Similarly article can be abbreviated as "art." and "arts." wherever used in a statute/code.
- To refer to an unnumbered paragraph or subdivision, use symbol "¶"or "para." to indicate a singular paragraph and use "¶¶" or "paras." to indicate multiple paragraphs.

2.2 Constitutional Statutes

2.2.1 *General Form: Constitution*

Name of the Act,	Year,	Pinpoint
The Constitution of India,	1950,	Art. 15.

2.2.2 *General Form: Constitutional Statutes*

Name of the Act,	Year,	Object of the Act/Act title,	Pinpoint
The Constitution (First Amendment) Act,	1951,	An Act to Amend the Constitution of India,	s. 7.
The Appropriation (No. 3) Act,	1996,	Act No. 31 of 1996,	s. 4.
The British Statutes (Repeal) Act,	2004,	Act No. 17 of 2004,	s. 2.
The Emblems and Names (Prevention of Improper Use) Act,	1950,	Act No. 12 of 1950,	s. 3.
The Representation of the People Act,	1951,	Act No. 43 of 1951,	s. 2.

- General rules stated above for the central statutes also apply to the Constitution and constitutional statutes.
- When referring to Constitutional Amendments, state the short object of the Amendment Act and not the Act title.
- For other Constitutional statutes, state the Act title of the statute. In case, a statute does not provide an Act title, simply state the official short title in italics followed by a non-italicized comma and a non-italicized year, *e.g. The Representation of the People Act*, 1951, s. 5.

2.3 General Form: Bills

Number,	Title of the Bill,	Name of the State (where applicable),	Year,	Pinpoint,	(Stage of the Bill).
Bill No. XX-F of 2009,	*The Constitution (One Hundred and Ninth Amendment) Bill,*		2009,	s. 2,	(as passed by the Houses of Parliament on 4 August 2009).
Bill No. CXXVII of 2005,	*The Prevention and Control of Infectious and Contagious Diseases in Animals Bill,*		2005,	s. 2(d),	(as passed by the Houses of Parliament on 25 February 2008).
Bill No. XLVII of 2008,	*The Gram Nyayalayas Bill,*		2008,	s. 9,	(as Passed By The Houses of Parliament on 22 December 2008).
Bill No. VI of 2009,	*The Industrial Disputes (Amendment) Bill,*		2009,	s. 4,	(pending, introduced in Rajya Sabha on 26 February 2009).
Bill No. XLVIII of 2008,	*The Pesticides Management Bill,*		2008,	s. 22,	(pending, introduced in Rajya Sabha on 21 October 2008).
Bill No. 98 of 2007,	*The Rehabilitation and Resettlement Bill,*		2007,	s. 25,	(lapsed, introduced in Lok Sabha on 6 December 2007).

Bill No. 65 of 2007,	*The Trade Marks (Amendment) Bill,*		2007,	s. 9,	(lapsed).
Bill No. 97 of 2006,	*The Judges (Inquiry) Bill,*		2006,	s. 10,	(lapsed, introduced in Lok Sabha on 19 December 2006).
Bill No. XXIX of 2005,	*The Standards Of Weights And Meas-ures (Enforcement) Amendment Bill,*		2005,	s. 7,	(withdrawn, introduced in Rajya Sabha on 10 March 2005).
Bill No. LX of 2004,	*The Scheduled Castes, Scheduled Tribes and Other Backward Classes (Reservation in Posts and Services) Bill,*		2004,	s. 2(c),	(replaced by a new bill, introduced in Rajya Sabha on 22 December 2004).
Draft Bill,	*The Nyaya Panchayats Bill,*		2006,	s. 6.	
Draft Bill,	*The National Health Bill,*		2009,	s. 2(m).	
Draft Bill,	*The Protection of Women against Sexual Harassment at Workplace Bill,*		2007,	s. 3.	
Draft Bill,	*Kerela State Land Policy Bill,*	Kerela,	2007,	s.2.	

- A Bill becomes an Act after being passed by both Houses of Parliament and after receiving Presidential assent.
- The Bill number should be provided in all cases, except draft bills.
- The title/heading of the Bill should be used to refer to the Bill while citing it as a source of information. Use of short title should be completely avoided in the case of Bills.
- Where referring to a State/provincial Bill/draft Bill, the name of the State should be provided after the title of the Bill/draft Bill.
- Any reference to a Bill must indicate the stage at which the Bill stands. Examples of five kinds of status of a bill have been given above: passed, lapsed, pending, withdrawn and replaced by a new bill.

- While providing the stage/status of the Bill, date of passing/ introduction shall be provided where possible. The date of final passing by either house shall be considered to be the date of passing a Bill. *E.g. The Constitution (One Hundred and Ninth Amendment) Bill* was passed by Rajya Sabha on 3 August, 2009 and by Lok Sabha on 4 August 2009. In this case, 4 August, 2009 will be treated as the date of passing of the Bill. Similarly, *The Prevention and Control of Infectious and Contagious Diseases in Animals Bill* was passed by Lok Sabha on 20 February, 2009 and by Rajya Sabha on 25 February, 2009. In this case, 25 February, 2009 will be treated as the date of passing of the Bill.
- Full Text/status of the Bills could be verified from www.prsindia.org

2.4 General Form: Regulations/Rules

Official Short Title of the Rules/Regulations,	Year,	Name of the State where applicable,	Pinpoint
The Protection of Women From Domestic Violence Rules,	2006,		r. 7.
The Medical Termination of Pregnancy Rules,	2003,		r. 9.

- **Abbreviate regulations to 'reg.' and rules to 'r.'.**

2.5 General Form: Ordinances

Title of the Ordinance,	Year,	Name of the State where applicable,	Name of Publishing Authority and Date of publication of the ordinance (where possible),	Number of Gazette,	Part of Gazette,	Section,	Pinpoint the clause
The Central Universities Ordinance,	2009,		The Gazette of India 15 January, 2009,	11,	II,	I,	cl. 5.
The Competition (Amendment) Ordinance,	2009,		The Gazette of India, 14 October, 2009,	40,	II,	I,	cl. 2.

- Complete title of the Ordinance should be provided.
- The information pertaining to the number of gazette, section and part of gazette should be provided.
- While pinpointing the clause, abbreviate clause to 'cl.' and provide page number where possible, *e.g.* 'cl. 5 at p. 2.'

2.6 General Form: Rules of Court

Short Title,	Year,	Name of State where applicable,	Pinpoint the rule.
The Supreme Court Rules,	1966,		r. 5.
The Delhi High Court (Right to Information) Rules,	2006,	Delhi,	r. 6.
Gujarat State Judicial Service Rules,	2005,	Gujarat,	r. 3.

- Abbreviate rule to 'r.'.

2.7 General Form: Orders

Short Title,	Year,	Name of State where applicable,	Pinpoint the order.
The High Courts (Punjab) Order,	1947,	Punjab,	o. 3.

- Abbreviate order to 'o.'.

2.7.1 United Kingdom

A. General Form: Legislations

Title,	Jurisdiction,	Chapter (c.),	Pinpoint
Anti-terrorism, Crime and Security Act, 2001,	UK,	c. 24,	s. 13.
Legal Aid Act, 1988,	UK,	c. 34,	s. 20.
Crime (International Co-operation) Act, 2003,	UK,	c. 32,	s. 7.
Housing Act, 2001,	Scot,	c. 10,	s. 42.
Justice and Security Act, 2007,	NI,	c. 6,	s. 14.

B. Rules

- Italicize the official short title (including the year) of the statute, if available, and place a non-italicized comma after the short title.
- If a statute does not provide an official short title, the title found at the head of the statute should be provided when making the first reference to the statute. Use "The" only if it forms the part of the title.

- If the short title is brief, it may also be used in subsequent references (*e.g.* the *Copyright Act*).
- If a statute has no official short title, or if the official short title is too long for subsequent references, a distinctive short title should be created and indicated in brackets at the end of the citation.
- Indicate jurisdiction after the title and place a comma after the same. 'UK' should be included after reference to the title of the statutes enacted by the United Kingdom Parliament. 'Imp' may be used to indicate that the statute was enacted by the Imperial Parliament. 'Scot' may be used to indicate the statutes enacted by the Scottish Parliament. "NI' may be used to indicate the statutes enacted by the Northern Ireland Assembly.
- For Statutes enacted by UK Parliament or Scottish Parliament or Northern Ireland Assembly, the chapter number of the statute should appear after the jurisdiction.
- Any pinpoint reference should follow the chapter number and should be preceded by a comma.

C. General Form: Bills

Title of the Bill,	Year,	Pinpoint,	Stage of the Bill	(history or last proceedings)
Academies Bill,	2010-2011,	s. 6,	Committee stage: House of Lords, 21-6-2010	(2nd reading: House of Lords, 7-6-2010).
Identity Documents Bill,	2010-2011,	s. 7,	Committee Stage: House of Commons, TBA	(2nd reading: House of Commons, 9-6-2010).
Representation of the People (Undue Influence) Bill,	2009-2010,	s. 1(2),		(1st reading: House of Commons, 10-3-2010).
Draft Bill, *Construction Contracts Bill,*	2008,	s. 2.		

D. Rules

- A Bill becomes an Act on receiving royal assent after being passed by House of Commons and House of Lords.
- An italicized title/heading of the Bill should be used to refer to the Bill while citing it as a source of information. Where a Bill provides short title, it may be used.

- The year in which the said Bill is before either House of Parliament should be provided. A comma should precede the reference to the year.
- Pinpoint the relevant section of the Bill. A comma should precede any reference to the relevant sections or paragraphs.
- Any reference to a Bill must indicate the stage at which the Bill stands.
- While providing the stage of the Bill, date of such stage should be provided, where possible. Where such date is undecided, indicate TBA for "to be announced".
- Brief history of the Bill should be provided within parenthesis.
- Full Text/status of the Bills could be verified from www.parliament.uk

E. Government Publications: United Kingdom

E.1 Command Papers: Command Papers are papers presented to the UK Parliament by Command of Her Majesty. Barring a few exceptions, they are published in a numbered series. The current series of the command papers uses prefix 'Cm'. The command paper series include State papers, white papers, green papers, government response to committee reports, reports of royal commission, statistics and reports of some government bodies, etc. Command papers should be cited as follows:

Author,	*Title,*	Command Paper Series	(Year)	Pinpoint.
United Kingdom,	*Countering International Terrorism: The United Kingdom's Strategy,*	Cm 6888	(2006)	at ¶49.

E.2 House Papers

Author,	*Title,*	House Paper Series Number,	Session	(Year)	Pinpoint.
Comptroller and Auditor General,	*Ministry of Defence: Progress in Combat Identification,*	HC 936,	Session 2005-2006	(2006)	at ¶13.

2.7.2 *Canada*

A. General Form: Legislations

Title,	Statute Volume	Jurisdiction	Year,	Chapter,	Pinpoint.
Family Day Act,	RS	A	2000,	c. F-4,	s. 12.
International Transfer of Offenders Act,	S	C	2004,	c. 21,	s. 15.
Young Offenders Act,	RS	NWT (Nu)	1988,	c. Y-1,	s. 20.

B. Rules

Title

- The short title of the statute should be italicized and followed by a comma.

Statute Volume

- Provide a citation to the Revised Statutes or Re-enacted Statutes (RS) or the Federal or Sessional volumes (S).

Jurisdiction

- Provide the abbreviated form of the jurisdiction of respective States as follows:

The following abbreviations for Canadian jurisdictions should be used:

Canada	C
Lower Canada	LC
Upper Canada	UC
Alberta	A
British Columbia	BC
Manitoba	M
New Brunswick	NB
Newfoundland	N
Northwest Territories	NWT
Nova Scotia	NS
Nunavut	Nu
Ontario	O
Prince Edward Island	PEI
Province of Canada	Prov C
Quebec	Q
Saskatchewan	S
Yukon Territory	Y

Year

- Provide the year of the enactment after the jurisdiction. A comma should follow the year.

Chapter

- The chapter number of the statute should be abbreviated to 'c.' and included.

Pinpoint

- Any pinpoint reference should follow the chapter number and should be preceded by a comma.

C. General Form: Bills

Bill no.,	Title of the Bill,	Year(,)	Pinpoint,	(Stage of the Bill).	(history or last proceedings)
C-24,	*An Act to Amend the Tobacco Products, Control Act,*	1996	at 4,	Committee Report: House of Commons, 11-12-1996	(2nd Reading: House of Commons, 4-6-1996).
S-1,	*An Act Relating to Railways,*			1st Reading: Senate, 26-1-2009.	
S-8,	*Tax Conventions Implementation Act,*	2009,	s. 6,	Passed: Senate, unknown	1st Reading: (Senate, 18-11-2009).

D. Rules

- A Bill becomes an Act on receiving royal assent after being passed by House of Commons and the Senate.
- Provide the Bill number followed by a comma. The Bill no. begins with 'C' for Bills introduced in the House of Commons and with 'S' for Bills introduced in the Senate.
- An italicized title/heading of the Bill should be used to refer to the Bill while citing it as a source of information. Where a Bill provides short title, it may be used.
- The year in which the said Bill is before either House of Parliament should be provided. A comma should precede the reference to the year.
- Pinpoint the relevant section of the Bill. A comma should precede any reference to the relevant sections or paragraphs. If pinpointing a particular page, use of comma after the year should be avoided.
- Any reference to a Bill must indicate the stage at which the Bill stands.

- While providing the stage of the Bill, date of such stage should be provided, where possible. Where such date is undecided, indicate TBA for "to be announced" or "unknown".
- Brief history of the Bill should be provided within parenthesis.
- Full Text/status of the Bills could be verified at www.parl.gc.ca

2.7.3 *Australia*

A. General Form: Legislation

Title	*Year*	(Jurisdiction)	Pinpoint
Aged Care Act,	*1997*	(Cth)	s.8.
Police Act,	*1990*	(NSW)	s.30.
Domestic and Family Violence Protection Act,	*1989*	(Qld)	s.11.

B. Rules

Title

- The short title of the statute should be italicized.

Year

- Italicize the year of the enactment and place it after the title. A comma should precede the year.

Jurisdiction

- Provide the abbreviated form of the jurisdiction in parenthesis. The abbreviations of respective jurisdictions in Australia are as follows:

Commonwealth	Cth
New South Wales	NSW
Queensland	Qld
South Australia	SA
Tasmania	Tas
Victoria	Vic
Western Australia	WA
Australian Capital Territory	ACT
Northern Territory	NT

Pinpoint

- Any pinpoint reference should follow the chapter number and should be preceded by a comma.

C. General Form: Bills

Title	*Year*	Pinpoint	Status
Healthcare Identifiers Bill,	2010,	s. 10,	Introduced: Senate, 15-3-2010.
Australian National Preventive Health Agency Bill,	2009,	s. 5,	2nd Reading: Senate, 28-10-2009.

D. Rules

- A Bill becomes an Act on receiving assent after being passed by House of Representatives and the Senate.
- An italicized title/heading of the Bill should be used to refer to the Bill while citing it as a source of information. Where a Bill provides short title, it may be used.
- The year in which the said Bill is before either House of Parliament should be provided. A comma should precede the reference to the year.
- Pinpoint the relevant section of the Bill. A comma should precede any reference to the relevant sections or paragraphs.
- Any reference to a Bill must indicate the stage at which the Bill stands.
- While providing the stage of the Bill, date of such stage should be provided, where possible. Where such date is undecided, indicate TBA for "to be announced" or "unknown".
- Status of the Bills could be verified at www.aph.gov.au

2.7.4 *New Zealand*

A. General Form: Legislation

Name of the Act,	Year,	Pinpoint.
Abolition of the Death Penalty Act,	1989,	s. 4.
Sale of Goods Act,	1908,	s. 49.

B. Rules

Title

- The short title of the statute should be italicized and followed by a comma.

Year

- Provide the year of the enactment after the title. A comma should follow the year.

Pinpoint

- Any pinpoint reference should follow the chapter number.

C. General Form: Bills

Title	*Year*	Pinpoint	Status
Border Security Bill,	2003,	s. 5,	2nd Reading: House of Representatives, 20-5-2004.
Domestic Violence Reform Bill,	2009,	s.16,	Introduced: House of Representatives, 30-9-2008.

D. Rules

- A Bill becomes an Act on receiving royal assent after being passed by the House of Representatives.
- An italicized title/heading of the Bill should be used to refer to the Bill while citing it as a source of information. Where a Bill provides short title, it may be used.
- The year in which the said Bill is before either House of Parliament should be provided. A comma should precede the reference to the year.
- Pinpoint the relevant section of the Bill. A comma should precede any reference to the relevant sections or paragraphs.
- Any reference to a Bill must indicate the stage at which the Bill stands.
- Status of the Bills could be verified at www.parliament.nz

2.7.5 *United States*

A General Form: Legislation/Code

Name of the Statute, (optional)	Volume or Title	Name of Code	Pinpoint	(Year of code)
Copyrights Act,	17	USC	§ 1301	(2009).
Public Contracts Act,	41	USC	§§ 601-603	(2009).

B. Rules

Name of the Statute

- It is not mandatory to provide the name of the statute. However, if it is provided, the name of the statute should be italicized. A comma should follow the name of the statute.

Statute Volume/Title/Chapter

- Provide the volume/title/chapter number of the referred legislation.

Name of the Code

- A code is the collection of statutes arranged according to subject matter. The US Code is a consolidation and codification by subject matter of the general and permanent laws of the United States. It does not include regulations issued by executive branch agencies, decisions of the Federal courts, treaties, or laws enacted by State or local governments. The abbreviations of some of the current official codes are as follows:

Federal	USC
Alabama	ALA CODE
Alaska	ALASKA STAT (Michie)
Arizona	ARIZ REV STAT
Arkansas	ARK CODE ANN (Michie)
California	CAL [subject] CODE (West)
	CAL [subject] CODE (Deering)
Colorado	COLO REV STAT
Connecticut	CONN GEN STAT
Delaware	DEL CODE ANN
District of Columbia	DC CODE ANN
Florida	FLA STAT
Georgia	GA CODE ANN
Hawaii	HAW REV STAT
Idaho	IDAHO CODE (Michie)
Illinois	ILL COMP STAT
Indiana	IND CODE
Iowa	IOWA CODE
Kansas	KAN STAT ANN
Kentucky	KY REV STAT ANN (Banks-Baldwin)
	KY REV STAT ANN (Michie)
Louisiana	LA REV STAT ANN (West)
Maine	ME REV STAT ANN (West)
Maryland	MD CODE ANN [subject]
Massachusetts	MASS GEN LAWS
Michigan	MICH COMP LAWS
Minnesota	MINN STAT
Mississippi	MISS CODE ANN
Missouri	MO REV STAT
Montana	MONT CODE ANN

Nebraska	NEB REV STAT
Nevada	NEV REV STAT
New Hampshire	NH REV STAT ANN
New Jersey	NJ STAT ANN (West)
New Mexico	NM STAT ANN (Michie)
New York	NY [subject] LAW (McKiinney)
	NY [subject] LAW (Consol)
	NY [subject] LAW (Gould)
North Carolina	NC GEN STAT
North Dakota	ND CENT CODE
Ohio	OHIO REV CODE ANN (Anderson)
	OHIO REV CODE ANN (West)
Oklahoma	OKLA STAT
Oregon	OR REV STAT
Pennsylvania	PA CONS STAT
Rhode Isląnd	RI GEN LAWS
South Carolina	SC CODE ANN (Law
Co-op) South Dakota	SD CODIFIED LAWS (Michie)
Tennessee	TENN CODE ANN
Texas	TEX CODE ANN (Vemon)
Utah	UTAH CODE ANN
Vermont	VT STAT ANN
Virginia	VA CODE ANN (Michie)
Washington	WASH REV CODE
West Virginia	W VA CODE
	WVA CODE ANN (Michie)
Wisconsin	WIS STAT
Wyoming	WYO STAT ANN (Michie)

Pinpoint

- Any pinpoint reference should follow the abbreviated name of the code. Use § to refer to a single section and §§ to refer to more than one section.

Year

- Provide the year of the code within parenthesis after the pinpoint reference.

C. General Form: Bills

D. Rules

3
CASE-LAW

3.1 General Forms: India

The citation methodology for case-laws in India largely depends upon the format followed by the reporter. Therefore, it is important to follow the citation format of the reporter as closely as possible to make it easier for the reader to locate the source.

3.1.1 General Form Some Reporters

Name of Parties,	Year	(Volume) if applicable	Abbreviated Name of the Reporter	Page number at which the case is appearing in the reporter	Pinpoint	Additional/ Optional Information
Banchhanidhi Singh alias *Nani Singh v. State of Orissa,*	1990		Cr LJ	397	at 399.	
Varghese @ Biju, S/o Mathai v. *State of Kerala,*	2007	(2)	KLT	644	at 649	(Kerela High Court).
State of Maharashtra v. *Deepti Anil Devasthali and Leena Anil Devasthali,*	2008	(110)	Bom LR	3643	at 3645	(Bombay High Court).
Palaniswamy Vaiyapuri v. *State,*	1966	(68)	Bom LR	941	at 941.	
Labhu Laxman v. *State of Gujarat,*	1999	(1)	GLR	889	at 890	(Gujarat High Court).

3.1.2 General Form for Delhi Law Times

Name of Parties,	Volume (Year)	Abbreviated name of the Reporter	Page number at which the case is appearing in the reporter	Pinpoint	Additional/ Optional Information
State v. *Balroop Singh,*	49 (1993)	DLT	644	at 645	(DB).

3.1.3 General Form for All India Reporter

Name of Parties,	Abbreviated name of the Reporter	Year	Jurisdiction	Page number at which the case is appearing in the reporter	Pinpoint	Additional/ Optional Information
Ram Naresh Yadav v. *State of Bihar,*	AIR	1987	SC	1500	at 1551.	
Hussainara Khatoon v. *Home Secretary, State of Bihar,*	AIR	1979	SC	1360	at 1379	(fair and speedy trial)
Mathai Thommen v. *State,*	AIR	1959	Ker	241	at 249.	
Palaniswamy Vaiyapuri v. *State,*	AIR	1968	Bom	127	at 128	(DB).

3.1.4 General Form for Criminal Law Journal

Janardhan Reddy v. *State of Hyderabad,*	(1951) 52	Cr LJ	736	at 739	(Supreme Court).

3.1.5 General Form for Supreme Court Cases

Bani Singli v. *State of Uttar Pradesh,*	(1996) 4	SCC	720	at 722.

State of Maharashtra v. Manubhai Pragaji Vashi,	(1995) 5	SCC	730	at 734.

3.1.6 General Form for Electronic Resources

Electronic Databases generally provide their own citation formats. Where the citation of no other official or unofficial reporter is available, the citation of the electronic database can be used.

Name of Parties,	Abbreviated name of the reporter/	Jurisdiction/	Page number/	Year	(Optional information)
State of U.P. v. *Kapil Das,*	MANU/	SC/	0266/	1972.	
Boota Ram v. *State of Punjab,*	MANU/	PH/	0316/	2007.	

3.1.7 General Form: No Official/Unofficial/Electronic Publisher

When referring to a case for which no citation of any official/unofficial/electronic publisher is available, complete information of the source should be provided.

Name of the Parties,	Criminal/civil appeal No./writ petition No.,	Date on which the case was decided,	Jurisdiction.
Rahul Ulhas Pise and Dhondiram Balkrishna Pise v. *The State of Maharashtra,*	Criminal appeal Nos. 231, 249 and 630 of 1988,	Decided on 3.8.2009,	Bombay HC (DB).

3.2 Rules

3.2.1 Name of the Parties

- If the name of the parties is mentioned in the text, do not repeat it in the footnotes. In such a case, only the citation is required.
- The names of the parties should be italicised, including the abbreviation 'v.' for versus.
- Provide complete names of the parties wherever possible. However, if the name is too long use the first name of the party in case of persons and provide complete name of the company but abbreviate "Company" as Co., "Limited" as Ltd. etc. in case of corporations.
- Capitalize the first alphabet of the name of the parties and the first letter of all the words, except prepositions and conjunctions.

- Where more than one person is on either side of the action, only first person's name should be used.
- Abbreviate Union of India to "UOI" and "State of ..." to "State" if required. If the name of the other party is not too long, there is no need to abbreviate the same.

3.2.2 *Abbreviated name of the Reporter*

- Abbreviated name of the reporter should be provided. See Appendix I for abbreviations of various reporters.
- In case of Supreme Court decisions, it is preferable to provide a citation from Supreme Court Cases (SCC).
- In case of State High Court decisions, it is preferable to provide a citation from All India Reporter (AIR).

3.2.3 *Year and Volume*

- The information pertaining to the year in which the reporter published a decision should be provided. If the year when decision was rendered is different from the year of publication, the same can be mentioned in additional/optional information.
- Where the reporter provides for a volume number, it shall be provided. Volume number should always follow the year in parenthesis.

3.2.4 *Jurisdiction*

- The name of the court should be provided either in citation or as optional information following citation. Further information regarding the bench deciding the case can be provided in optional/ additional information, such as, Division Bench, Full Bench, etc.

3.2.5 *Page number*

- Indicate the number of first page of the decision in the reporter.

3.2.6 *Pinpoint*

- Always place the pinpoint reference after the first page of the decision in the reporter.
- Use "at" before the pinpoint.
- Paragraph pinpoints may be added after page pinpoint, *e.g.*

Ram Naresh Yadav v. *State of Bihar*,	AIR	1987	SC	1500	at 1551,	¶12.

3.2.7 *Parallel Citations*

- Provide parallel citations where possible, especially if no SCC or AIR citation is available.
- Parallel citations should be separated with colon *e.g.*

State of Rajasthan v. *Bhagwana Ram*, 2002 (5) WLC 369 (370): 2002 (4) WLN 569 (571).

3.3 General Form: District Courts

In the absence of any official/unofficial/electronic reporter for orders and judgments of district courts, complete information of the source should be provided.

3.3.1 Criminal Cases

Name of the parties, Abbreviated Case, Identification Number if available, Serial Number if available, First Information Report number (FIR No.) if available, Name of Police Station where case was registered if available, date of judgment/order, nature of proceedings, the name of the Judicial Officer, designation of Judicial Officer *i.e.* whether ASJ, MM or ACMM etc., jurisdiction (central, south, etc.), Delhi.

- The name of the parties should be italicized.
- Case Identification Number should be provided depending upon the nature of the proceedings. Following are some of the examples of nature of proceedings in Trial Courts alongwith their abbreviations:

Case Identification Number	Abbreviated Case Identification Number
Sessions Case Number 69/2001	SC No. 69/01
Court Record Number 31/2002	CR No. 31/02
Criminal Appeal Number 21/2008	Crl. Appeal No. 21/08
Criminal Revision Number 100/2009	Crl. (R.) No. 100/09
Criminal Miscellaneous Application	Crl. (M.) App. No. 23/99 Number 23/1999
Complaint Case Number 71/2003	CC No. 71/03
Corruption Case Number 121/1993	Corruption Case No. 121/93

- Serial Number should be provided where available and should be abbreviated as "Serial No.".
- First Information Report Number should be provided where available and should be abbreviated as "FIR No.".
- Name of Police Station where case was registered should be provided either in full or abbreviated where available.
- Date of judgment or order should be provided and abbreviated as DOJ in case of judgment and DOO in case of order.
- It is optional to provide a brief introduction to the nature of proceedings.
- Full Name of the Judicial Officer deciding the case should be provided followed by his/her designation.

- Jurisdiction of the District Court should be provided.
- All the information should be separated by comma.

Illustrations

State v. *Surender Kumar*, FIR No. 188/08, NDLS, Sessions Case, DOJ 21.11.2009, Poonam Chaudhary, ASJ, Central, Delhi.

State v. *Veerpal*, SC No. 69/01, FIR No. 583/2000, Rohini, Sessions Case, DOJ 30.11.2009, Virender Kumar Goel, ASJ, Fast Track Court, West, Delhi.

Sh. Naved Yar Khan v. *State*, Crl. (R.) No. 100/09, Criminal Revision, DOJ 23.10.2009, Madhu Jain, ASJ, North, Delhi.

Mr. Sumit v. *State*, Crl. Appeal No. 21/08, Criminal Appeal, DOJ 10.11.2009, Dharmesh Kr. Sharma, ASJ, North, Delhi.

Wildlife v. *C. Manoharan*, FIR No. 440/09, Bail Application, DOO 9.11.2009, Dig Vinay Singh, ACMM, Central, Delhi.

Texaco v. *Jagdish*, CC No. 171/03, Complaint Case, DOO 19.11.2009, Dig Vinay Singh, ACMM, Central, Delhi.

CBI v. *O.P. Bhatia*, Corruption Case No. 121/93, Corruption Cases, DOO 31.10.2009, V.K. Maheshwari, Special Judge-03, PCA, CBI, Delhi.

State v. *Ved Singh*, FIR No. 873/96, Serial No. 560/01, Nangloi, Criminal Case, DOJ 8.10.2009, Gaurav Rao, MM, West, Delhi.

Sita Ram Gupta v. *Ravinder Kumar Nagpal*, CC No. 61/04, Serial No. 1035/04, Preet Vihar, Complaint Case, DOJ 26.10.2009, Vivek Kumar Gulia, MM, East, Delhi.

Sita Ram Gupta v. *Ravinder Kumar Nagpal*, CC No. 61/04, Serial No. 1035/04, Preet Vihar, Order on Sentence, DOO 29.10.2009, Vivek Kumar Gulia, MM, East, Delhi.

State v. *Sandeep*, FIR No. 534/05, Welcome, Criminal Case, DOJ 12.11.2009, Shuchi Laler, MM, Mahila Court, East, Delhi.

Smt. Kaushar Bano v. *Zubeda*, CC No. 80/07, Domestic Violence case, DOJ 6.11.2009, Shuchi Laler, MM, Mahila Court, East, Delhi.

State v. *Mohd. Anwar*, SC No. 78/2007, FIR No. 94/2004, Welcome, Narcotics Drugs and Psychotropic Substances Case, DOJ 23.11.2009, Sudesh Kumar, ASJ, Special Judge, NDPS Act, North-East, Delhi.

3.3.2 *Civil Cases*

> *Name of the Parties,* Case Identification Number, Nature of Proceedings, Date of Judgment/Order/Award, the name of the Judicial Officer, designation of Judicial Officer *i.e.* whether ADJ or Civil Judge etc., jurisdiction (central, south, etc.), Delhi.

- Case Identification Number should be provided depending upon the nature of the proceedings. Following are some of the examples of nature of proceedings in civil courts alongwith their abbreviations:

Case Identification Number	Abbreviated Case Identification Number
Suit Number 252/1998	Suit No. 252/98
Miscellaneous Application Number 268/2009	M.A. No. 268/09
Regular Civil Appeal Number 369/2006	RCA No. 369/06
Miscellaneous Civil Appeal Number 06/2003	Misc. CA No. 06/03
Guardianship Petition Number 207/2007	GP No. 207/07
Mental Health Application Number 11/2009	MHA No. 11/09
Land Acquisition Case Number	LAC No.
Industrial Dispute Number	ID No.
Petition Number	Pet. No.
Rent Control Case Number	E- or ARCT No.
Probate Number	PC No.

- Date of judgment or order or award should be provided and abbreviated as DOJ in case of judgment, DOO in case of order and DOA in case of award.
- It is optional to provide a brief introduction to the nature of proceedings.
- Full Name of the Judicial Officer deciding the case should be provided followed by his/her designation.
- Jurisdiction of the District Court should be provided.
- All the information should be separated by comma.

Illustrations

> *M/s Bee Kay Engineering & Contractors* v. *BSES Rajdhani Power Ltd.,* Suit No. 252/98, Declaration, Permanent and Mandatory Injunction, DOJ 25.11.2009, Tyagita Singh, Civil Judge, North Delhi.
>
> *Mrs. Basanti Sidha* v. *M/s Juju Finance & Leasing Ltd.,* Suit No. 256/03, Suit For Recovery of Arrears of Rent, DOJ 05.12.2009, Loveleen, Civil Judge, Central Delhi.

Mohsin Khan v. *Jitender Kumar,* M.A. No. 32/09, DOO 17.11.2009, Kamlesh Kumar, AD&SJ, Central Delhi.

M/s ICICI Bank Ltd. v. *Mr. Anish Khurana,* Suit No. 114/09, Suit For Recovery, DOJ 20.11.2009, Kamlesh Kumar, AD & SJ, Central Delhi.

The Delhi Stock Exchange Association Ltd. v. *Major Rampat,* RCA No. 06/08, Regular Civil Appeal, DOJ 24.11.2009, Dinesh Bhatt, ADJ, North Delhi.

Smt. Kamla Sung v. *Amar Nath Sharma,* MCA No. 01/09, Misc. Civil Appeal, DOJ 16.11.2009, Ajay Goel, SCJ Cum RC, Central Delhi.

Baby Ishita v. *Chaudhary Randhir Singh,* GP No. 74/09, Guardianship, DOO 10.11.2009, V.P. Vaish, DJ, North Delhi.

Sardar Parminder Singh v. *State,* PC No. 127/06, Probate, DOJ 17.11.2009, V.P. Vaish, DJ Cum ASJ, North Delhi.

Dr. Rakesh Vakil v. *Smt. Renu Vakil & Ors.,* M.H.A. No. 11/09, Mental Health Case, DOJ 19.11.2009, V.P. Vaish, DJ Cum ASJ, North Delhi.

Nand Kumar Sharma v. *Smt. Surya Kanta,* ARCT No. 28/09, Rent Control Case, DOJ 24.11.2009, V.P. Vaish, DJ Cum ASJ, Addl. Rent Control Tribunal, North Delhi.

Mohd. Sayeed v. *Abdul Salam,* E-410/04, Rent Control Case, DOJ 23.11.2009, Raghubir Singh, Addl. Rent Controller, East Delhi.

Sh. Vijay Arora v. *State,* Pet. No. 497/07, Succession Petition, DOJ 16.11.2009, Sanjeev Kumar Singh, Adm. Civil Judge, Central Delhi.

Smt. Munni Devi v. *Bijender Singh & Ors.,* Suit No. 771/07, Motor Accident Claim, DOA 18.11.2009, Rajiv Mehra, Presiding Officer, Motor Accident Claim Tribunal, East Delhi.

The Workman Shri Mahavir Bhandari v. *The Management of M/s Pressure Cooker,* ID No. 38/09, Labour/Industrial Dispute, DOA 12.11.2009, Sh. Sukhdev Singh, AD & SJ, Presiding Officer, Labour Court No. VII, Delhi.

Dhir Singh v. *UOI,* LAC No. 122/08/07, Land Acquisition Case, DOJ 12.11.2009, Ashwani Sarpal, ADJ, North-West Delhi.

3.4 Case-Law: International

3.4.1 United Kingdom

A. General Form: United Kingdom

Examples:

Style of cause	[Year] Volume	Abbreviated name of the reporter	Starting page (court)	Pinpoint
Thomas v. *Peter*	[1999]	AC	594 (HL)	at 45.
Mark v. *Anthony*	[2007] 124	NLJ	60 (QB)	at 12.

B. Rules

Name of the parties

- The names of the parties should be italicised, including the abbreviation 'v.' for versus.
- Provide complete names of the parties wherever possible. However, if the name is too long use the first name of the party in case of persons and provide complete name of the company but abbreviate "Company" as Co., "Limited" as Ltd. etc., in case of corporations. Capitalize the first alphabet of the name of the parties and the first letter of all the words, except prepositions and conjunctions.
- Where more than one person is on either side of the action, only first person's name should be used.

Year and Volume

- The information pertaining to the year in which the reporter published a decision should be provided in square brackets.
- Where the reporter provides for a volume number, it shall be provided.

Abbreviated name of the Reporter

- Abbreviated name of the reporter should be provided.
- The *Law Reports*, which are published by the Incorporated Council of Law Reporting for England and Wales, should be cited where possible. The abbreviation for some of the series in the *Law Reports* are as follows:

Queen's and King's Bench	(1952-)	QB
	(1901-51)	KB
	(1891-1900)	QB
	(1875-90)	QBD
	(1865-75)	LRQB
Common Pleas	(1875-80)	CPD
	(1865-75)	LR CP

Exchequer	(1875-80)	Ex D
	(1865-75)	LR Ex
Chancery	(1891-)	Ch
	(1875-90)	Ch D
Equity	(1865-75)	LR Eq
Family	(1972-)	Fam
Appeal Cases	(1890-)	AC
	(1875-90)	App Cas
Privy Council	(1865-75)	LRPC
Probate and Divorce	(1891-1971)	P
	(1875-90)	PD
	(1865-75)	LR P&D
Admiralty and Ecclesiastical Cases	(1865-75)	LR Adm & Eccl

Page number

- Indicate the number of first page of the decision in the reporter.

Jurisdiction

- Indicate the name of the court before the pinpoint. Use '(QB)', '(Ch)', and '(F)' for the divisions of the High Court. The Commercial Court within the QBD is '(Com Ct)'. A Scottish case in the House of Lords is indicated by (HL Sc). Citations before 1865 do not require the court, nor do citations that include a neutral citation.

Pinpoint

- Use "at" before the pinpoint.
- Paragraph pinpoints may be added after page pinpoint, e.g.

Thomas v. *Peter* [1999] AC 594 (HL) at 45 ¶ *12.*

C. Neutral Citations: United Kingdom

Judgments of the United Kingdom courts are available with neutral citations on British and Irish Legal Information Institute website (www.bailii.org)

Neutral citations provide the names of the parties, year of judgment, court and case number. When providing neutral citations, a parallel citation of an authentic reporter should also be provided, if possible. When citing an unreported decision, indicate 'unreported' in parenthesis after the neutral citation.

Following are some examples of neutral citations:

R. v. *A,* [2001] UKHL 25: [2001] 3 All ER 1.

Homecastle & Ors. v. *R,* [2009] UKSC 14: [2010] 2 WLR 47.

Christian & Ors. v. *The Queen,* [2006] UKPC 47: [2007] 2 WLR 120.

D. Nominate Reports: United Kingdom

The nominate reports were published commercially under the name of the reporter between 1537-1865. A parallel citation should be provided where possible. The *English Reports* are preferred over the *Revised Reports.* e.g.

Peter v. *Jones,* [1857] 2 H&N 564: 157 ER 232.

Stanley v. *Henry,* [1952] 9 Hare 627: 68 ER 664.

3.4.2 *Canada, Australia and New Zealand*

A. General Form: Canada

Style of Cause	[Year]	Volume	Abbreviated Name of the Reporter	Starting Page	Pinpoint
R. v. *Lavallee*	[1990]	1	SCR	852	at 857.
R. v. *Gladue*	[1999]	1	SCR	688	at 690.
R. v. *Gilpin*	[2002]		BCSC	1876	at 1877.

B. General Form: Australia

Style of Cause	[Year]	Volume	Abbreviated Name of the Reporter	Starting Page	Pinpoint
R. v. *Hugh*	[2000]	202	CLR	525	at 530.
DPP v. *Silbert*	[2000]	112	A Crim R	88	at 90.
Thomas. v. *The Queen*	[2009]	179	ALR	73	at 78.

C. General Form: New Zealand

Style of Cause	[Year]	Volume	Abbreviated Name of the Reporter	Starting Page	Pinpoint
Richard Donald Collins v. *The Queen*	[2010]	1	NZLR	30	at 35.
The Queen v. *Heidi Maria Greenfield*	[2002]	1	NZLR	15	at 17.

D. Common Rules

Name of the parties

- The names of the parties should be italicised, including the abbreviation *'v.'* for versus.

- Provide complete names of the parties wherever possible. However, if the name is too long use the first name of the party in case of persons and provide complete name of the company but abbreviate "Company" as Co., "Limited" as Ltd. etc., in case of corporations. Capitalize the first alphabet of the name of the parties and the first letter of all the words, except prepositions and conjunctions.
- Where more than one person is on either side of the action, only first person's name should be used.

Year and Volume

- The information pertaining to the year in which the reporter published a decision should be provided in square brackets.
- Where the reporter provides for a volume number, it shall be provided.

Abbreviated name of the Reporter

- Abbreviated name of the reporter should be provided.
- Official Reporters are preferred over unofficial reporters.
- In the absence of any official or unofficial reporter, it is also permissible to use the citation format of the Legal Information Institute in the following manner:

Examples of:	Style of Cause	[Year]	Abbreviated Name of the Court	Starting Page, Paragraph Pinpoint	(Name of the Legal Information Institute)
Canada	*R.* v. *Milijevic*	[2010]	ABCA	115, ¶ 10	(CanLII).
Australia	*R.* v. *Lavender*	[2005]	HCA	37, ¶21	(AustLII).
New Zealand	*The Queen* v. *Heidi Maria Greenfield*	[2002]	NZCA	12, ¶¶15-18	(NZLII).

Page number

- Indicate the number of first page of the decision in the reporter.

Pinpoint

- Use "at" before the pinpoint.
- Paragraph pinpoints may be added after page pinpoint, *e.g.*

3.4.3 *United States of America*

Style of Cause	Volume	Reporter Series and Series Number	Starting Page, Pinpoint	(Court, Year)
Florida v. *Scott,*	120	L.Ed. 2d	415, 425	(Supreme Court, 1999).
ABC Bus Co. v. *Mass Transport Corp.,*	930	F.2d.	220, 230	(3rd Cir., 2000).
XYZ Mills v. *United States,*	500	F.2d.	30, 38	(Fed. Cir., 2001).

Name of the parties

- The names of the parties should be italicised, including the abbreviation *'v.'* for versus followed by a comma.
- Provide complete names of the parties wherever possible. However, if the name is too long use the first name of the party in case of persons and provide complete name of the company but abbreviate "Company" as Co., "Limited" as Ltd. etc., in case of corporations. Capitalize the first alphabet of the name of the parties and the first letter of all the words, except prepositions and conjunctions.
- Where more than one person is on either side of the action, only first person's name should be used.

Volume and Reporter

- The Volume number of the Reporter series should follow the case name.
- Abbreviated name of the reporter should be provided.

Starting Page and Pinpoint

- The starting page of the decision should be provided.
- A comma should precede any pinpoint reference.

Court and Year

- Abbreviated form of the court should appear in parenthesis.

Federal Courts: Reference to the decision of Supreme Court does not require the name of the court. The Court of Appeals are referred to by the numbered circuit (1st Cir., 2nd Cir., etc.). The US Court of Appeals for District of Columbia is cited as 'DC Cir.' and the US Court of Appeals for Federal Circuit is cited as 'Fed. Cir.'

State Courts: The abbreviations for the highest courts are as follows:

Alabama Supreme Court	Ala
Alaska Supreme Court	Alaska
Arizona Supreme Court	Ariz
Arkansas Supreme Court	Ark
California Supreme Court	Cal
Colorado Supreme Court	Colo
Connecticut Supreme Court	Conn
Delaware Supreme Court	Del
Florida Supreme Court	Fla
Georgia Supreme Court	Ga
Hawaii Supreme Court	Haw
Idaho Supreme Court	Idaho
Illinois Supreme Court	Ill
Indiana Supreme Court	Ind
Iowa Supreme Court	Iowa
Kansas Supreme Court	Kan
Kentucky Supreme Court	Ky
Louisiana Supreme Court	La
Maine Supreme Judicial Court	Me
Maryland Court of Appeals	Md
Massachusetts Supreme Judicial Court	Mass
Michigan Supreme Court	Mich
Minnesota Supreme Court	Minn
Mississippi Supreme Court	Miss
Missouri Supreme Court	Mo
Montana Supreme Court	Mont
Nebraska Supreme Court	Neb
Nevada Supreme Court	Nev
New Hampshire Supreme Court	NH
New Jersey Supreme Court	NJ
New Mexico Supreme Court	NM
New York Court of Appeal*	NY
North Carolina Supreme Court	NC
North Dakota Supreme Court	ND
Ohio Supreme Court	Ohio
Oklahoma Supreme Court	Okla

Oregon Supreme Court	Or
Pennsylvania Supreme Court	Pa
Rhode Island Supreme Court	RI
South Carolina Supreme Court	SC
South Dakota Supreme Court	SD
Tennessee Supreme Court	Twin
Texas Supreme Court	Tex
Utah Supreme Court	Utah
Vermont Supreme Court	Vt
Virginia Supreme Court	Va
Washington Supreme Court	Wash
West Virginia Supreme Court of Appeals	W Va
Wisconsin Supreme Court	Wis

- Year

The information pertaining to the year in which the reporter published a decision should be provided within parenthesis after the reference to the court. A comma should precede reference to the year.

4
GOVERNMENT DOCUMENTS

4.1 Debates and Proceedings

Legislature,	*Type of Debate,*	Title,	Date,	Session,	Part,	Name of the the Speaker
Lok Sabha,	Government Bill	*Introduction of the Insurance Regulatory and* Bill, *Development Authority Bill, 1999,*	(28th October, 1999),	Session-I,	Part-II,	Mr. Yashwant Sinha and Mr. Somnath Chatterjee.
Lok Sabha,	Special Mention,	*Uproar over the issue of laying of Jain Commission Report alongwith Action Taken Report laid on the table on 20.11.1997,*	(24th November, 1997),	Session VI,	Part-II,	Mr. A.C. Jos.

- Indicate whether referring to a debate in Lok Sabha Assembly or Rajya Sabha Assembly.
- Provide information on the type of debates.
- Italicize the title of the debate.
- Provide date, session and part number of the proceedings. Additional information can be provided in brackets after part number, *i.e.* (24th November, 1997), Session VI, Part-II (Monsoon Session), Mr. A.C.Jos.
- Refer to www.parliamentofindia.nic.in to provide the complete details pertaining to the proceedings.
- Since it is not possible to provide a pinpoint to the relevant text as the proceedings are not in a paragraph form, it is important to indicate the name of the speaker whose debate is being referred to

in your article/paper. Therefore, the name of the speaker here neither refers to the appointed speaker of the Parliamentary proceedings nor to the participant who introduced the topic for debate. It essentially refers to the participant whose comments/ submissions are being referred to in your article/paper. If you are referring to two participants/speakers, please provide names of both the speakers.

4.2 Reports of Committees

- The citation format for Parliamentary Committees, departmentally related standing committees and *ad hoc* committees is similar, with the exception of indicating whether the committee is Parliamentary or *ad-hoc* or standing committee.
- Indicate the name of the legislature alongwith a brief sessional information, *i.e.* twelfth Lok Sabha, thirteenth Lok Sabha, etc.
- Italicize the title of the report and provide the number/volume of the report followed by the date of presentation in that particular Legislature.
- If the report is divided into page numbers and paragraphs, pinpoint both. If the report does not provide for page number of the relevant text, pinpoint the paragraph.
- Additional information, such as <URL> of the online source can be provided after the pinpoint and before the full-stop/period, *i.e.* online: Indian Parliament < www.parliamentofindia.nic.in/ls/>.

4.2.1 *Parliamentary Committees*

Legislature,	Name of the Parliamentary, Committee,	*Title of the Report,*	Number/ Volume of Report,	(Date of presentation),	Pinpoint,	Online: Name of Web Page <URL>
Fourteenth Lok Sabha,	Parliamentary Committee on Empowerment,	*Scheme for Women Rehabilitating Woman in Circumstances Swadhar,*	8th Report,	(11th August, 2006),	at 9, para 43,	online: Indian Parliament< www. parliamentofindia. nic.in/-ls/>.
Fourteenth Lok Sabha,	Parliamentary Committee on the Welfare of Scheduled Castes and	*Reserve Bank of India – Credit facilities provided by the Nationalised*	22nd Report,	(27th April, 2007),	at 24, para 2.12.	

	Scheduled Tribes,	*Banks to the Scheduled Castes and Scheduled Tribes*			

4.2.2 *Departmentally Related Standing Committees*

Legislature,	Name of the Standing Committee,	*Title of the Report,*	Number/Volume of Report,	Date of presentation,	Pinpoint
Fourteenth Lok Sabha,	Standing Committee on Food, Consumer Affairs and Public Distribution,	*Demands for Grants (2007-2008),*	18th Report,	(27th April, 2007),	at 65, para 3.78.
Fourteenth Lok Sabha,	Standing Committee on Social Justice and Empowerment (Ministry of Tribal Affairs),	*Action taken by the Government on the Recommendations/ Observations contained in the Thirty-third Report of the erstwhile Standing Committee on Labour and Welfare on 'The Tribal Cooperative Marketing Development Federation of India Limited (TRIFED)'*	3rd Report,	(22nd December, 2004),	at 12, para 1.19.

4.2.3 Ad-Hoc *Committees*

Legislature,	Name of the *Ad Hoc* Committee,	*Title of the Report,*	Number/Volume of Report,	Date of presentation,	Pinpoint
Thirteenth Lok Sabha,	*Ad Hoc* Railway Convention Committee,	*Construction of New Gauge Line between Kolayat and Phalodi on strategic construction,*	3rd Report,	(18th December, 2001),	at paras 35, 36.

5
INTERNATIONAL LAW SOURCES

5.1 Documents

5.1.1 International Treaties

The following format is applicable for multilateral, bilateral and other international/state specific treaty series.

Title	Parties (if applicable)	Opened for signature on,	Treaty,	Series,	Other information (optional)
European Convention for the Protection of Human Rights and Fundamental Freedoms,		4 November 1950,	213 U.N.T.S. 221 at 228,		[ECHR].
International Covenant on Civil and Political Rights,		19 December 1966,	999 U.N.T.S. 171, arts. 10-13,		(accession by India on 10 April 1979).
Optional Protocol to the International Covenant on Civil and Political Rights,		19 December 1966,	999 U.N.T.S. 171 at 178,		(India has not signed the optional protocol).
Convention on the Elimination of All Forms of Discrim-ination against Women,		1 March 1980,	1249 U.N.T.S. 13,		(India signed on 30 July 1980 and ratified on 9 July 1993).

General Agreement on Tariffs and Trade,		30 October 1947,	55 U.N.T.S. 187,	(entered into force 1 January 1948) [GATT 1947].
Tashkent Declaration,	India and Pakistan,	10 January 1966,	560 U.N.T.S. 8166,	registered (on 22 March 1966).
Agreement on South Asian Free Trade Area,		6 January 2004,	Online: SAARC <www.saarc-sec.org>,	(entered into force 1 January 2006).
Memorandum of Under-standing Between India and Thailand on the Collaboration of Information Technology and Services,		28 November 2001,	Online: Ministry of External Affairs <meaindia.nic.in>.	
Agreement between the India and China on the Political Parameters and Guiding Principles for the settlement of India-China Boundary Question,		11 April 2005,	Online: Ministry of External Affairs <meaindia.nic.in>.	

- Provide the complete title of the treaty/agreement in Italics. When the names of the signatories appear in the title of a treaty, shorten them to reflect common usage (*e.g.* "India" and not "the Government of the Republic of India".
- If the names of the parties to a bilateral treaty are not already mentioned in the title, provide the names of the parties after the title. If the names of the parties are already provided in the title, there is no need to provide the names again. *See* above illustrations.
- Provide the date when the treaty was signed or opened for signature.

- Provide the treaty series/agreement citation after the date. Refer to treaty series in the following order of preference: (1) *United Nations Treaty Series* (U.N.T.S.) or *League of Nations Treaty Series* (L.N.T.S.) in the order Volume Number U.N.T.S. Page Number at Article Number if pinpointing; (2) Official treaty series of a State involved (*e.g. United Kingdom Treaty Series* (U.K.T.S.)); (3) Other sources of international treaties (*e.g. International Legal Materials* (I.L.M.)). It is also permitted to provide the online citation of a multilateral or bilateral treaty if the citation to United Nations Treaty Series is not available. For online citation, provide the name of the website followed by URL. *See* illustration above.
- Additional information may be provided at the end of the citation, *e.g.* the names of the parties to a multilateral treaty, the date of entry into force, the number of ratifications, and the status of particular countries, etc.

5.1.2 United Nations Documents

5.1.2.1 Constitutive Documents

Constitutive Documents should be cited as follows:

Charter of the United Nations, art. 51.

Statute of the International Court of Justice, art. 65(1).

5.1.2.2 Resolutions, Decisions, Reports

Format for Resolutions/s Decisions/s Reports	Author (if applicable)	*Title,*	UN body's Resolution or Decision Number) if available,	Session number or year if available,	Supp. No. if available	UN doc. No. if available,	date,	Pinpoint.
Resolution		*Universal Declaration of Human Rights,*	UNGA Res. 217 (III),	3rd Sess.,	Supp. No. 13,	UN Doc. A/810	(1948),	71.
		Declaration of Independence to Colonial Countries and Peoples,	UNGA Res. 1514 (XV),				(14 December 1960).	

			UNSC Res. 1373,			UN Doc. S/RES/1373,	(28 September 2001).	
	ECOSOC,	*Enlargement of the Commission on Human Rights and the Further Promotion of Human Rights and Fundamental Freedoms,*				Res. 1990/48,	(25 May 1990).	
Decision		*Protection of the Heritage of Indigenous People,*	UNESC Dec. 1998/277,	1998,	Supp. No. 1,	UN Doc. E/1998/98,		113 at 115.
Reports	Commission on Crime Prevention and Criminal Justice,	*Report on the Ninth Session,*	UNESC,	2000,	Supp. No. 10,	UN Doc. E/2000/30.		
	UNCHR,	*Report of the Working Group on Arbitrary Detention,*				UN Doc. E/CN.4/1992/20,	(21 January 1992).	
	UNCHR,	*Report of the Special Rapporteur on Torture,*				UN Doc. E/CN.4/1986/15,	(1986).	
		Report of the UN Commissioner for Refugees,	UNGA	15th Sess.,	Supp. No. 11,	UN Doc. A/4378/Rev.1	(1960).	

	ILC,	*Report of the International Law Commission on the Work of its 42nd Session,*		UN Doc. A/ 45/ 10,	(1 May 20 July 1990).
Notes and Comments	UNCHR,	*Comment on Egypt's Second Periodic Report on the implementation of the ICCPR,*		UN Doc. CCPR/ C/79/ Add. 23,	(9 December 1993).
	UN Committee for the Elimination of All Forms of Discrimination against Women,	*Note by the Secretariat, Compilation of General Comments and General Recommendations Adopted by Human Rights Treaty Bodies,*		UN Doc./ HRI/ GEN/ 1/Rev. 1,	(29 July 1994)

- Provide the title in italics. For reports, cite the author if not mentioned in the title. It is optional to cite the resolution titles.
- For decisions and resolutions, provide the abbreviated name of the UN Body (*e.g.* UNGA for UN General Assembly, UNSC for UN Security Council) alongwith the decision or resolution number if available after the title. Provide the session number and supplement number if available.
- If neither the session number nor supplement number is available, it is imperative to provide the UN Document Reference Number followed by the date/year of the document in parenthesis.
- Pinpoint if required by using art. for article, arts. for articles, s. for section, ss. for sections, sub-s. for sub-section, sub-ss. for sub-

sections, para. for paragraph, paras. for paragraphs, sch. for schedule, schs. for schedules, app. for appendix.

- In citing the documents, the following commonly used words should be abbreviated:

Word	Abbreviation
Decision	Dec.
Document	Doc.
Emergency	Emer.
Meeting	Mtg.
Mimeograph(ed)	Mimeo.
Number	No.
Official Records	OR
Plenary	Plen.
Recommendation	Rec.
Regulation	Reg.
Resolution	Res.
Session	Sess.
Special	Spec.
Supplement	Supp.

5.1.3 *Diplomatic Conferences*

Title	Document Reference Number,	Date.
Final Act of the UN Diplomatic Conference of Plenipotentiaries on the establishment of an International Criminal Court,	UN Doc. A/CONF. 183/10,	(17 July 1998).

5.1.4 *United Nations Year Books (U.N.Y.B.)*

Abbreviated name of UN Body,	*Title,*	(Year)	U.N.Y.B	Page Number	Pinpoint
UNGA,	*Questions relating to International Terrorism,*	(1972)	U.N.Y.B.	649	at 651.

5.2 European Union

5.2.1 Documents of European Union

The regulations, directives, decisions, debates, and other documents of European Union are published in the *Official Journal of the European Union.* The *Official Journal* consists of two related series (the L series for legislation and the C series for information and notices) and a supplement (the S series for public tenders which is available only in electronic format as of 1st July, 1998). To cite any of the regulations, decisions, or other documents, follow the following format:

Prefix EC as author	*Title,*	Citation.
EC,	*Commission Regulation No.1361/2000 of 27th June, 2000 Amending Representative Prices and Additional Duties for the Import of Certain Products in the Sugar Sector,*	[2000] O.J.L. 155/45
EC,	*Explanatory Note Concerning Annex III of the EU Mexico Agreement,*	[2004] O.J.C. 40/2
EC,	*Decision of the Council and of the Commission of 17th November, 2009 on the conclusion of a Partnership and Cooperation Agreement establishing a partnership between the European Communities and their Member States, of the one part, and the Republic of Tajikistan, of the other part,*	[2009] O.J.L. 350/1.
EC,	*Prior Notification of a Concentration(Case COMP/M 4712 — ERG/IPM/ISAB Energy Services) — Candidate Case for Simplified Procedure,*	[2007] O.J.C. 150/ 10.

- Prefix "EC" for "European Community" followed by italicized title of the document.
- The citation format consists of the year in brackets [ ], followed by the "L" or "C" series issue number for that particular year/the page number of the document in that series. Indicate the O.J. series, then the issue number and the first page of the instrument, separated by

a slash (*e.g.* L 15/45). Please note that the series number is not the same as volume number. For more information access to the official journal (from 1998 onwards) on to www.eur-lex.europa.eu.

5.2.2 *Court of Justice of the European Communities*

The decisions of Court of Justice of European Communities are published in the Reports of Cases before the Court of Justice, the Court of First Instance and Civil Service Tribunal (all abbreviated to ECR).

Name of the Parties,	Case Identification Number	Citation if available or date	Pinpoint.
Sector Photo Group v. *Van Raemdonck,*	(C-45/08)	(23 December 2009).	
Carlos Arauzo Burillo v. *Commission of the European Communities,*	(F-67/07)	[2007] ECR 00000.	
SAEME v. *OHMI - Racke (REVIAN's),*	(T-407/05)	[2007] ECR II-04385.	
SITA EcoService Nederland BV, formerly Verol Recycling Limburg BV v. *Minister van Volkshuisvesting, Ruimtelijke Ordening en Milieubeheer,*	(C-116/01)	[2003] ECR I-02969 at 02971.	

- Begin with the italicized names of the parties.
- Provide the case identification number in parenthesis. The case identification number will begin with "C" if it is an order/judgment of the Court, with "T" if it is an order/judgment of the Court of First Instance and with "F" if it is an order/judgment of Civil Service Tribunal.
- If citing a recent case, it may be possible that the bibliographic information pertaining to the page number in ECR may not be available. In such a situation, the complete date should be provided within parenthesis.
- Where the bibliographic information pertaining to page numbers in ECR is available on the aforementioned website, the same should be provided in the format: [year] ECR page number. Citations to the judgments of the Court since 1990 should include prefix "I-page number" to indicate the cases decided by the Court of Justice and

prefix "II-page number" to indicate the cases decided by the Court of First Instance. *See* above illustrations.

5.2.3 *European Court of Human Rights*

5.2.3.1 *Before 1 November, 1998*

Name of Parties,	Date,	Paragraph Number (if judgment),	*Reporter/ Series*	Year	Volume
Delta v. *France,*	30 January 1990,	§ 38,	*Series A No. 191-A.*		
Allenet de Ribemont v. *France* (interpretation),	7 August 1996	§ 17,	*Reports of Judgments and Decisions*	1996-	III.
Gautrin v. *France* (friendly settlement),	20 May 1998,	§ 57	*Reports*	1998-	III.

5.2.3.2 *After 1st November, 1998*

The form of citation for decisions and judgments published after 1st November, 1998 is as follows:

Name of Parties,	Application number,	Paragraph Number (if judgment)	ECHR	Year-	Volume
Campbell v. *Ireland,*	No. 45678 /98,	§ 24,	ECHR	1999-	II.
Campbell v. *Ireland* [GC],	No. 45678 /98,	§ 24,	ECHR	1999-	II.
Campbell v. *Ireland*(dec.),	No. 45678 /98,.	§ 24,	ECHR	1999-	II
Campbell v. *Ireland*(dec.) [GC],	No. 45678/ 98,	§ 24,	ECHR	1999-	II.

- Provide italicized names of the parties. In the absence of any indication to the contrary the cited text is a judgment on the merits delivered by a Chamber of the Court. Any variation from that is added in brackets after the name of the case:

  "[GC]" is added if the judgment or decision has been given by the Grand Chamber of the Court. "(dec.)" for a decision on admissibility, "(preliminary objections)" for a judgment concerning only preliminary objections, "(just satisfaction)" for a judgment concerning only just satisfaction, "(revision)" for a judgment concerning revision, "(interpretation)" for a judgment concerning interpretation, "(striking out)" for a judgment striking the case out, or "(friendly settlement)" for a judgment concerning a friendly settlement.

5.2.4 *European Commission for Human Rights*

Decisions of European Commission for Human Rights were published in *Collection of Decisions* prior to 1974 and in *Decisions and Reports* prior to 1998 (both abbreviated to Eur. Comm. HR).

Illustration:

Yarrow Plc v. *United Kingdom*, (1983) 30 Eur. Comm. HR 155 at 179.

5.3 Inter-American Court of Human Rights

5.3.1 *Judgments and Advisory Opinions*

	Style of cause/title	(Year of judgment),	Type of decision and no.,	Reporter	Case or report no.,	Pinpoint.
Judgments	*Case of Boyce et al.* v. *Barbados*	(2007),		Inter-Am. Ct. H.R. (Ser. C)	No. 169,	at para. 47
Advisory Opinions	*Article 55 of the American Convention on Human Rights*	(2009),	Advisory Opinion OC-20/09, H.R. (Ser. A)	Inter-Am. Ct.	No. 20,	at para. 24.

- Begin with the style of cause.
- Provide the date of the decision in parentheses.
- Specify if the document is an advisory opinion and provide the advisory opinion number.
- Provide the reporter and case number. The Inter-American Court of Human Rights publishes judgments in *Inter-American Court of Human Rights, Series C: Decisions and Judgments* and advisory opinions in *Inter-American Court of Human Rights, Series A: Judgments and Opinions.*

Inter-American Commission on Human Rights

Style of cause	(Year of judgment),	Inter-Am. Comm. H.R.	Case or report no.,	Pinpoint,	Annual report,	Document number (year of document).
Moreno v. *Argentina*	(2009),	Inter-Am. Comm. H.R.	No.83/09,		*Annual Report of the Inter-American Commission on Human Rights: 2008-2009,*	OEA/Ser.L/V/II./doc.51 (2009).

- Begin with the style of cause followed by the year of decision in parentheses.
- Indicate "Inter-Am. Comm. H.R." followed by the case or report number.
- Decisions of the Inter-American Commission on Human Rights are published in the commission's annual reports. Cite the commission's annual report and the document number. The document number starts with the letters OEA (not OAS) whatever the language of the document.

5.4 International Economic Materials (GATT and WTO)

	GATT or WTO,	*Title,*	Dec., Rec., or Doc. number	Sess., session number,	B.I.S.D.	online.
Decisions and recommend-ations		*Accession of Guatemala,*	GATT C.P. Dec. L/6824,	47th Sess.,	38th Supp. B.I.S.D. (1991) 16.	
Reports	GATT,	*Committee on Anti Dumping Practices- Semi Annual Report under Article16.4 of the Agreement -India- Corrigendum,*	GATT Doc. G/ADP/N/ 145/IND/ Corr.1,			(18 December. 2006)
	WTO,	*Working Party on the Accession of the Former Yugoslav Republic of Macedonia - Accession of the Former Yugoslav Republic of Macedonia - Implementation of the WTO Agreement on Technical Barriers to Trade (TBT),*	WTO Doc. WT/ACC/ 807/11 (2000),			online: WTO <http://docsonline .wto.org>.

Meetings and Communica-tions	WTO, General Council,	*Enlargement of European Union- Communication from Argentina,*	WTO Doc. WT/GC/ W/559,	online: WTO<http://docs-online.-wto.org>.

- Decisions and recommendations do not have an author. GATT and WTO are the authors of all reports.
- Give the decision, recommendation, or document number. If none, give the full date of the decision or recommendation. Abbreviate "Contracting Parties" to "C.P.", "Decision" to "Dec.", and "Recommendation" to "Rec."
- Cite GATT documents to the *Basic Instruments and Selected Documents* (B.I.S.D.) if possible, followed by the year in parentheses and the first page of the document.

5.5 International Courts & Tribunals

5.5.1 *Judgments, Orders and Advisory Opinions of Permanent Court of International Justice (1922-1946)*

	Names of parties,	(year),	Type of decision,	Reporter	Case no.	Pinpoint.
Judgments	*Case concerning certain German interests in Polish upper Silesia,*	(1925),		P.C.I.J. (Ser. A)	No. 6	at 18.
Advisory Opinions	*Competence of the International Labour Organization to regulate, incidentally, the personal work of the Employer,*	(1926),	Advisory Opinion,	P.C.I.J. (Ser. B)	No. 13	at 3.
Orders	*The Borchgrave* case,	(1937),	Order,	P.C.I.J. (Ser. A/B)	No. 72	at 172.

- Italicize the names of the parties/short or long title of the case.
- Provide the year of the decision/order in parentheses after the style of cause.
- Specify if the document is an order or an advisory opinion.
- Provide the P.C.I.J. series followed by the case number. Please refer to www.worldcourts.com for more information on citation.

5.5.2 *Judgments, Orders and Advisory Opinions of International Court of Justice (1946-present)*

I.C.J. judgments, opinions, or orders not yet printed may be cited to the I.C.J. website <www.icj-cij.org> according to the Internet citation rules.

	Style of cause names of parties,	Type of decision,	year of reporter	Reporter	First Page	Pinpoint
Judgments	*Fisheries Jurisdiction Case (Spain* v. *Canada),*	Jurisdiction of the court,	[1998]	I.C.J. Rep.	432.	
Orders	*Legality of Use of Force (Yugoslavia* v. *United States of America), Provisional Measures,*	Order of 2 June 1999,	[1999]	I.C.J. Rep.	916.	
Advisory Opinions	*Legal Consequences of the Construction of a Wall in the Occupied Palestinian Territory,*	Advisory Opinion,	[2004]	I.C.J. Rep.	136.	
	Reparations for Injuries suffered in the service of United Nations,	Advisory Opinion,	[1949]	I.C.J. Rep.	174	at 177.

- Provide the names of the parties/title in italics.
- Specify if the document is an order or an advisory opinion. If referring to an order, provide the full date.
- Provide the year of the reporter in brackets, followed by the reporter and the first page.
- Pinpoint, if required.

5.5.3 *International Criminal Tribunals*

Following are the guidelines for citing documents created by the International Criminal Court, the International Criminal Tribunal for the former Yugoslavia, the International Criminal Tribunal for Rwanda, the Special Court for Sierra Leone, and the Special Panels for Serious Crimes (East Timor), etc.

Name of the Parties,	Document reference No. or case No.,	Title of document	Date of document	Pinpoint	Tribunal,	Source.
Goring et. al.,	LT-19724,		(1 October 1946)	at page 172.	(The International Military Tribunal, Nuremberg, Germany),	Online: International Criminal Court <www.legal-tools.org>

Araki et. al.,	LT-19734,	Judgment	(12 November 1948)	at 1145	(International Military Tribunal for the Far East),	Online: International Criminal Court <www.legal-tools.org>
Prosecutor v. *Dusko Tadic,*	IT-94-1,	Judgment on Sentence Appeal	(26 January 2000)	at paras. 33-36	(International Criminal Tribunal for the Former Yugoslavia, Appeals Chamber),	Online: International Criminal Court <www.legal-org>
Prosecutor v. *Jean Paul Akayesu,*	ICTR-96-4,	Judgment	(1 June 2001)	at 155	(International Criminal Tribunal for Rwanda, Appeals Chamber),	Online: International Criminal Court <www.legal-tools.org>
Prosecutor v. *Momcilo Trajkovic,*	P. No. 17/02	Verdict	(28 November 2003)		(District Court of Gjilan, United Nations Mission in Kosovo),	Online: International Criminal Court <www.legal-tools.org>
Prosecutor v. *Omar Hassan Ahmad Al Bashir,*	ICC-02/05-01/09	Pre-trial	(24 June 2009)		(International Criminal Court, Pre-trial Chamber),	Online: International Criminal Court <www.legal-tools.org>

- Italicize the names of the parties. If there is one accused, write *Prosecutor* v. *Accused*. If there are multiple accused, use only the name of the first accused followed by *et. al.*

- The case number as provided on the website of International Criminal Court (legal-tools) should be provided. In the absence of a case number, document reference number can also be provided.
- The title of the document should provide a brief summary suggesting whether the document is a judgment/proceeding etc.
- The date of document is the date as it appears in the document, *i.e.* the date of judgment or the date of verdict, and not the date the document was published to the website.

6
SECONDARY SOURCES

6.1 Periodicals

6.1.1 Citation Format

Name of the Author (First name Last name),	"Title of the article"	(Year)	Volume	Abbreviated name of the Periodical/ Journal	First Page	Pinpoint
Ty S. Twibell,	"Immigrant Nations: A Comparison of the Immigration Law of Australia and the United States"	(2000)	19	U. Tas. L. Rev.	57	at 78.
Marc Galanter,	"Justice in many rooms: Private Ordering and Indigenous Law"	(1981)	19	J. Legal Pluralism	1	at 1-17.
Manu Aggarwal & Meera Kaura,	"Mediation in Penal Law"	(2005-2006)	II	DLR	15	at 19.
Hiram E. Chodosh, *et al.*	"Indian Civil Justice Reform: Limitation and Preservation of the Adversarial Process"	(1997-1998)	30	N.Y.U.J. Int'l & Pol.	1.	

6.1.2 Author

- Provide the First Name and Last Name of the Author followed by comma.
- Indicate the name of the Author as it appears in the article. Do not substitute initials where complete name is used and *vice versa*.

- In case a work has been authored by two persons, separate their names by using "&" between their names. *See* above illustration.
- In case a work has been authored by more than two persons, use the name of first author followed by *et al.*

6.1.3 *Title*

- Place the title in double quotation marks.
- Do not put comma after the title.
- Follow the spellings and grammar of the title as provided in the publication.
- Separate the title and subtitle with a colon": "*See* above illustrations.

6.1.4 *Year of publication*

- Place the year of publication of the journal/periodical in parenthesis *e.g.* (2004).
- Where the journal/periodical uses academic year to denote the year of publication, provide the reference to entire academic year, *e.g.* (2004-2005).

6.1.5 *Volume*

- If a journal/periodical is divided into volumes, provide the volume number of the journal/periodical which contains the referred article.
- If it is further sub-divided in issues and each issue begins from a fresh page, provide the issue number immediately after the volume number, separated by a colon.
- If the issue is further sub-divided in sub-issues, provide the same in parenthesis ( ) immediately after the issue number.

  e.g. Bernard S. Cohn, "Anthropological Notes on Dispute and Law in India" (1965) 67:6(2) Am. Anthropologist 82.

6.1.6 *Title of the Journal*

- Abbreviate the title of the journal according to list of abbreviations in Appendix-II. If the list of abbreviations does not contain the abbreviation for the referred journal, write the name of the journal in full.

6.1.7 *First page of the article*

- Provide the first page of the referred article after the abbreviated title of the journal.
- Do not provide the last page of the article, *e.g.* 23-46.

6.1.8 *Pinpoint*

- Place the reference to a particular page number after the first page number by using "at _" or "at 13-25".
- Do not use "page" or "p." before page numbers.

- If the article uses sub-divisions in paragraphs, it is preferable to also provide reference to the particular paragraph number, *e.g.* "at 43, ¶6" or "at 56, ¶¶ 19-21".
- Use symbol "¶"or "para." to indicate a singular paragraph and use "¶¶" or "paras." to indicate multiple paragraphs.

6.2 Books/Monographs

6.2.1 Citation Format

Name of the Author First Name Last Name,	If editor.	*Title of the Book*	Edition (optional)	(Place of Publication:	Name of Publisher,	Year of Publication)	Pinpoint
Paras Diwan,		*Law of Adoption, Minority, Guardianship & Custody,*	4th edn.	(New Delhi:	Universal Law Publishing Co. Pvt. Ltd.,	2010).	
J.S. Verma		*The New Universe of Human Rights*		(New Delhi:	Universal Law Publishing Co. Pvt. Ltd.,	2006).	
Alan R. Beals,		*Village India: Studies in the Little Community*		(Chicago:	University of Chicago Press,	1967)	at 15.
Howard S. Becker,		*Outsiders: Studies in the Sociology of Deviance*		(London:	Collier-Macmillan,	1973)	at 10.
M. Cappe-lletti & B. Garth ,	eds.	*Access to Justice: Emerging Issues and Perspectives I, II, III*		(Milan:	A. Giuffrè,	1979)	at 54.
Masaji Chiba,	ed.	*Asian indigenous law: In interaction with received law*		(London:	Routledge Internat-ional,	1986)	at 72.
Michael King *et al.,*		*Non-Adversarial Justice*		(Annadale:	Federation Press,	2009).	

6.2.2 *Author*

- Provide the First Name and Last Name of the Author followed by comma.
- Indicate the name of the Author as it appears in the article. Do not substitute initials where complete name is used and *vice versa*.
- In case a work has been authored by two persons, separate their names by using "&" between their names. *See* above *illustration*.
- In case a work has been authored by more than two persons, use the name of first author followed by *et. al.*
- Indicate editor's name before the title of a collection.
- Use "ed." or "eds." after the name of the editor(s) to indicate that they have edited the collection.
- If a work has been edited by two persons, separate their names by using "&" between their names. See above illustration.
- If a work has been edited by more than two persons, use the name of first editor followed by *et. al. See* above illustration.
- If one has revised the work of another, cite as follows:

  Satyajit A. Desai, *Mulla's Principles of Hindu Law*, 17th Edn., Vol. 1 (New Delhi: Butterworths, 1998).]

6.2.3 *Title*

- Italicize the title of the book.
- Do not put comma after the title unless followed by the information on edition and volume of the book.
- Follow the spellings and grammar of the title as provided in the publication.
- Separate the title and subtitle with a colon
- If the title of the work is in Hindi or any other language other than English, phonetically transcribe the title into English followed by an English translation of the title in brackets, *e.g.*

  C.K. Takwani, *Prashasanik Vidhi* [Administrative Law], 1st Edn., (New Delhi: Eastern Book Company, 2005).

6.2.4 *Edition and Volume Number*

- If the edition number of a monograph is known it should be provided after the title of the book. In such a situation, comma should follow the title of the book.
- If the book is divided into volumes, the volume number of the referred book should be provided after the edition number. If the edition number is not known, volume number should be provided after the title of the book.

Satyajit A. Desai, *Mulla's Principles of Hindu Law,* 17th Edn., vol. 1 (New Delhi: Butterworths, 1998).

- Do not place comma after the edition number unless followed by volume number.
- Do not place comma after volume number.

6.2.5 *Place of Publication*

- Indicate the place of publication as it appears on the title page or the verso of the title page.
- If there are more than one places of publication, use only the first place of publication.

6.2.6 *Name of Publisher*

- Indicate the complete name of the publisher as it appears on the title page or the verso of the title page.

6.2.7 *Year*

- Provide the year of the publication of the current (referred) edition.

6.2.8 *Pinpoint*

- Provide the pinpoint reference information after the publication information.
- To refer to a particular page number use "at 16" or "at 13-25".
- Do not use "page" or "p." before page numbers.
- To refer to a particular chapter or chapters, use "c." followed by the chapter number, *e.g.* c. III
- Do not use "at" before "c."
- If the chapter is further sub-divided in paragraphs, it is preferable to also provide reference to the particular paragraph number. Use symbol "¶"or "para." to indicate a singular paragraph and use "¶¶" or "paras." to indicate multiple paragraphs, *e.g.* "c. III at 43, ¶6" or "c. IV, ¶6".

6.3 Collection of Essays

6.3.1 *Citation Format*

Name of the Author,	"Title of the Essay"	in	Name of the Editor, (if applicable)	Ed.	*Title of the Book*	Publication Information	First page if known	Pinpoint.
Marc Galanter,	"The Aborted Restoration of 'Indigenous' Law in India"	in	Marc Galanter,	Ed.	*Law and Society in Modern India*	(Delhi: Oxford University Press, 1989)		at 49-51.

Catherine S. Meschievitz & Marc Galanter,	"In Search of Nyaya Panchayats: The Politics Moribund Institution"	in	Richard L. Abel.,	Ed.,	*The Politics of Informal Justice*	New York: (Academic Press, 1982)	1	at 23.

- Place the name of the author(s) and the title of the essay in double quotes before the reference to the collection.
- Use "&" to separate the names of two authors and "*et. al.*" with the name of first author in case of more than two authors.
- Use "in" before referring to the collection of essays.
- Provide the name of the editor(s) of the collection. Use "&" to separate the names of two editors and "*et al.*" with the name of first editor in case of more than two editors.
- Italicize the title of the collection followed by the publication information in parenthesis as in the case of monographs.
- Indicate the first page of the essay in the collection, if known.
- Pinpoint, if required.

6.4 Dictionaries

6.4.1 Citation Format

Title of the Dictionary,	Edition	Publication Information	"Key Word/ Searched term"
Black's Law Dictionary,	8th Edn.,		"*Ratio Decidendi*".
Webster's New World College Dictionary, New Millenium,	4th Edn.,	(Delhi: IDG Books India Pvt. Ltd., 2000)	"accused".

- Italicize the title of the dictionary.
- Indicate the edition or year.
- Provide publication information, if available.
- If referring to an online dictionary follow the following format:

  "word", online: Name of the website <website.address>

  "Partnership", online: Law Guru <www.lawguru.com>

6.5 Encyclopaedias

6.5.1 Citation Format

- The citation format for encyclopaedias is same as that of monographs excluding the name of the author *e.g.*

Halsbury's Laws of England, 1st Edn., Vol. 1 (London: Butterworths, 1907) at 45.

- Italicize the name of the encyclopedia followed by a comma,
- Provide the information partnership to the edition, followed by a comma, if the edition has more than one volumes.
- Provide information pertaining to volume number.
- Provide publication information within pertaining (place of publishing: name of publisher, year).
- Pinpoint the relevant page.

For online encyclopaedias follow the same format as online dictionaries *e.g.*

"Collateral estoppels", online: WEX, Cornell University Law School <www.topics.law.cornell.edu>

6.6 Book Reviews

6.6.1 Citation Format

Author, of Book Review	"Title of book review", (if applicable)	Book review of	Title of the book reviewed	by	Name of the author/ editor of the book reviewed	Citation information
Alka Chawla,		Book Review of	*Justice in Robes*	by	Ronald Dworkin	(2006-2007) XXVIII-XIX DLR 282.
Werner F. Menski,		Book Review of	*Asian Indigenous Law: In Interaction with Received Law*	by	Masaji Chiba, ed.	(1988) 37 Int'l & Comp LQ 750.

6.6.2 Rules

- Provide the complete name of the Author *i.e.* first name and the family name, followed by a comma.
- If the book review has a title, provide the same within double quotes.
- Provide the title of the book reviewed in italics, preceded by the term 'Book Review of', and followed by 'by' and the name of the author/editor of the book reviewed.
- Provide the citation information of the book review, *i.e.* same as journal articles.

6.7 Case Comments

6.7.1 Citation Format

Name of the Author,	"Title of the comment" (if applicable)	Nature of comment,	On	Name of the case (if not mentioned in the title)	Citation of case comment.
Gitanjali Nain Gill,	"Balancing Competing Values- *Development* v. *Environment*: A comment on *Intellectuals Forum Tirupathi* v. *State of A.P.*"	Case Comment,			(2005) XXVII DLR 214.

6.7.2 Rules

- Provide the complete name of the Author *i.e.* first name and the family name, followed by a comma.
- Provide the title of the comment within double quotes followed by "case comment on" and the name of the case, if not already mentioned in the title.
- Provide the citation information of the book review, *i.e.* same as journal articles.

6.8 Comments, Remarks and Notes

6.8.1 Citation Format

Name of the Author	"Title of the note/comment"	Type of document	Citation
Kamla Sankaran,	"Access to Justice: Some Reflections on the Role of Legal Education",	Note	(2006-2007) XXVIII-XXIX DLR 157.

6.8.2 Rules

- Provide the complete name of the Author *i.e.* first name and the family name, followed by a comma.
- Provide the title of the comment/note/remark within double quotes followed by a comma.
- Inform the reader whether it is a comment/note/remark followed by the citation information *i.e.* same as journal articles.

6.9 Unpublished Manuscripts

6.9.1 Citation Format

Author	*Title*	(Date of creation) if available	[unpublished	archived at	Location].
Manu Aggarwal & Meera Kaura,	*Project Report on Speedy Disposal of Less Serious Offences*	(2005)	[unpublished,	archived at	Law Commission of India Law Library]

6.9.2 *Rules*

- Provide the complete name of the Author *i.e.* first name and the family name, followed by a comma.
- Italicize the title of the manuscript.
- Provide the date/year of creation of the document within parenthesis.
- Indicate the location of the document within brackets, *i.e.* [unpublished, archieved at location].

6.10 Major Papers, Thesis and Dissertations

6.10.1 *Citation Format*

Author	*Title* Document and degree if available,	(Nature of the institution,	Name of	Year)	[unpublished].
Marie-Eve Sylvestre,	*Policing Disorder and Criminalizing the Homeless in Montreal and Rio de Janeiro: A critique of the Justifications for Repression in Law and Practice*	(Thesis, Law School,	Harvard	2007)	[unpublished].
Meera Kaura,	*Conflict Resolution and Access to Justice in Indian Villages: Are the three Indian Experiments a Gandhian legacy or Reverence to Common Law*	(LL.M, Major Research Paper,	University of Ottawa,	2007)	[unpublished].

6.10.2 *Rules*

- Provide the complete name of the Author *i.e.* first name and the family name, followed by a comma.
- Italicize the title of the paper/thesis.
- Provide the information pertaining to the document, *i.e.* whether thesis/paper, name of the institution and the year within parenthesis.
- Quote unpublished within brackets if the same has not been published anywhere.

6.11 Addresses and Papers delivered at Conferences

6.11.1 Citation Format

Name of the Author,	"Title/Topic of Presentation"	(Whether paper or lecture or address	Conference/Venue	Date)	[unpublished]. or citation.
Marc Galanter & Jayanth Krishnan,	"Debased Informalism: Lok Adalats and Legal Rights in Modern India"	(Paper presented at	the First South Asian Regional Judicial Colloquium on Access to Justice at New Delhi,	1-3th November, 2002)	[unpublished].
Justice R.C. Lahoti,	"Envisioning Justice in the 21st Century"	(Keynote Address delivered at	the Conference of the Chief Ministers of States and Chief Justices of High Courts at Vigyan Bhawan, New Delhi,	18th September, 2004),	(2004) 7 SCC (J) 13.
Hon'ble Justice S.B. Sinha,	"Judicial Reform in Justice-Delivery System"	(Speech delivered to	Sapru Law Institute at Allahbad, India,	27th March, 2004),	(2004) 4 SCC (J) 35.

6.11.2 Rules

- Provide the complete name of the Author *i.e.* first name and the family name, followed by a comma.
- Provide the title of the paper presented within double quotes.
- Provide the information pertaining to the nature of presentation followed by the conference venue and date within parenthesis.
- Provide the citation of the same or indicate unpublished within brackets if the same has not been published anywhere.

6.12 Newspapers

6.12.1 Citation Format: Signed

Name of the Author,	"Title"	*Name of the Newspaper,*	Place of publication if known	(Date of publication)	Pinpoint	Electronic source (if applicable).
Robert Mackey,	"Video and Blogging from Lahore under Attack"	*The New York Times,*	USA: New York	(28th May, 2010)		
Heather Timmons & Hari Kumar,	"India steadily increases its lead in Road Fatalities"	*The New York Times,*	USA: New York	(7th June, 2010)	Asia at A4.	www.nytimes.com

6.12.2 Citation format: Unsigned

"Title"	*Name of the Newspaper,*	Place of publication if known	(Date of publication)	Pinpoint	Electronic source (if applicable).
"U.S. to 'evaluate' Indian request to bring Anderson to Justice"	*The Hindu,*	New Delhi	(13th June, 2010)	at front page.	

6.12.3 Citation format: Untitled

Name of the Author,	Description of the piece,	*Name of the Newspaper,*	Place of publication if known	(Date of publication)	Pinpoint
Madhav Govind,	Letter to the Editor,	*The Hindu,*	New Delhi	(7th June, 2010).	

6.12.4 Rules

- Provide complete name of the author(s), *i.e.* first name and family name, followed by a comma in case of a signed and untitled article/report. If making a reference to the Editorial, the author should be cited as Editorial.
- If making a reference to an unsigned article/report, *i.e.* if the said article/report does not bear any name or merely states correspondent, start the citation with the title.
- Provide the name of the title within double quotes. If referring to the Editorial, and if the same has a title, it should be included. If referring to an untitled article/report/opinion, such as, a letter to the editor, notes or comments, etc., provide the description of the work in place of the title.
- Provide italicized name of the Newspaper. It should be followed by a comma if indicating the place of publication. However, if date of publication follows the name, the use of comma should be avoided.
- The place of publication should be provided. If referring to a newspaper outside India, the name of the country may be provided before the place of publication, *e.g.* United States of America or USA: New York, Australia: Sydney Morning Herald.
- The date of publication should be provided within parenthesis.
- Pinpoint the relevant page. The section of the newspaper where the article/report appears could also be indicated, such as, Asia at A4, Sports at A6, Business at Front Page, etc.

6.13 Interviews

6.13.1 Citation Format

Name of the Interviewer,	Interview with	The name of the interviewee Full date)	(location or form of interview)	Source/ Online: Name of the website <website address>
Charlie Rose,	Interview with	Dr. Manmohan Singh	(Charlie Rose Show, 27th February, 2006)	Online: Charlie Rose Show <www.charlierose.com>

6.13.2 Rules

- Provide the name of the interviewer followed by a comma and the term "Interview with".
- Provide the name of the interviewee.
- Provide the location and/or form of the interview along with the date of the said interview within parenthesis.
- Provide the web address, if available. If the interview seen on a TV Channel or heard on Radio, cite the source as: Broadcaster, "Title", *Name of the Program,* Full date and Pinpoint reference, if any. If the interview is published in a newspaper, cite the source in the same manner as newspaper report/articles.

6.14 Press Release

6.14.1 Citation Format

Title	(Press Release, Date)
Cabinet approves the Marriage Laws (Amendment) Bill, 2010 to amend the Hindu Marriage Act	(Press Release, 10th June, 2010).

6.14.2 Rules

- Provide the italicized title of the press release.
- Provide the date of the press release preceded by the term "Press Release".

6.15 Letters and Emails

6.15.1 Citation Format

Email or Letter from Author	to Recipient	(Place, if known: Full Date).
Letter from Thomas Macaulay	to Hannah M. Macaulay	(London: 14th June, 1833).
Letter from Lord Mountbatten	to Maharaja Hari Singh	(Kashmir: 27th October, 1947).
Email from Barrack Obama	to Li Liangzhang	(China: 9th June, 2010).

6.15.2 Rules

- Provide the name of the author, preceded by "letter from" or "email from" and succeeded by "to recipient".
- Indicate the place of receipt of such letter or email along with full date within parenthesis.

APPENDIX I

LIST OF INDIAN REPORTERS

Name of Reporter	Abbreviation
Accidents Claims Journal	A.C.J.
Accidents Judicial Report	A.J.R.
Accidents Compensation Cases	A.C.C.
Acadamy Law Review	ALR
Administrative Tribunal Cases	A.T.C.
Administrative Tribunals Law Times	A.T.L.T.
Air Force Law Review	A.F.L.R.
Administrative Tribunals Reporter	A.T.R.
Ajmer-Merwara Law Journal	A.M.L.J.
All India Arbitration Law Reporter	Arb LR
All India Cases	All Ind. Cas.
All India Civil Law Judgment	A.I.C.L.J.
All India Criminal Decision	A.I.C.D.
All India Criminal Law Reporter	All. Cri. L.R.
All India High Court Cases	A.I.H.C.
All India Hindu Law Reporter	A.I. Hin. L.Rtr.
All India Land Law Reporter	A.I.L.L.R.
All India Rent Control Journal	R.C.J
All India Reporter (Supreme Court)	A.I.R. (SC)
All India Reporter (Notes of Cases) (Any State)	AIR (N.O.C.) abbreviated name of the State
All India Reporter (Notes of Supreme Court Cases)	A.I.R (N.S.C)
All India Reporter (Notes of Unreported Cases)	A.I.R (N.U.C.)
All India Reporter Supreme Court Weekly All India Services Law Journal	A.I.R S.C.W. S.L.J.
All India Services Reports	All Serv. Rep.
All India Tribunal Cases	A.I.T.C.
All Indian Law Reports, Allahabad Series	All I.LR (All.)
All Maharashtra Law Reporter (Criminal)	All M.R (Cri).

All Maharashtra Law Reporter	All M.R.
All Pallisten Legal Decisions	P.L.D.
Allahabad Appeal Cases (Criminal)	All. A.C. (Cri).
Allahabad Civil Journal	All. C.J.
Allahabad Criminal Cases	All. Cr.C.
Allahabad Criminal Law Journal	All. Cr. L.J.
Allahabad Criminal Cases & Reports	Alld. Cr. & R.
Allahabad Criminal Reports	All. Cr. R.
Allahabad Criminal Rulings	All. Cri. Rul.
Allahabad Law Journal	All. L.J.
Allahabad Law Journal (Notes of Cases)	All. L.J. (N.O.C.)
Allahabad Law Reports	All. L.R.
Allahabad Law Times	All. L.T.
Allahabad Rent Cases	All. Ren. Cas.
Allahabad Tax Judgments	All. Tax J.
Allahabad Weekly Cases	All. W.C.
Allahabad Weekly Notes	All. W.N.
Allahabad Weekly Reporter	All. W. R.
Andhra Law Times	Andh. L.T.
Andhra Legal Decisions (Criminal)	Andh. L.D. (Cri).
Andhra Legal Decisions	Andh. L.D.
Andhra Pradesh Law Journal	A.P.L.J.
Andhra Pradesh Law Journal (Criminal)	A.P.L.J. (Cri).
Andhra Weekly Law Reporter	Andh. W.L.R.
Apex Decisions (Delhi)	A.D. (Del)
Apex Decisions (Supreme Court)	A.D.(SC)
Aps. Labour Cases	Aps. Labour Cases.
Arbitration and Conciliation Digest	Arb. & Con. Digest
Arbitration and Trade Mark Law Reporter	Arb. & T.M.L.R.
Arbitration Law Reporter	Arb. L.R.
Asia Law Review	Asia L.R.
Assam Law Reports	Assam L.R.
Banker's Journal	Bank. J.
Banking Cases	Bank. C.
Banking Commercial Law Reporter	Bank. C.L.R.
Banking Important & Selected Judgments	B.I.S.J.
Banking Law Judgment	Bank L.J.

Banking Law Reporter	Bank L.R.
Bar Council Journal	B.L.R.
Bengal Law Reports	Beng. L.R.
Bihar Bar Council Journal	B.B.C.J.
Bihar Criminal Cases	Bihar Cri. C.
Bihar Law Journal	Bih. L.J.
Bihar Law Journal Reports	B.L.J.R or Bihar L.J.R.
Bihar Law Judgments	B.L.J. or Bihar L.J.
Bihar Law Times (Reports)	B.L.T. (Rep) or Bihar L.T. (Rep).
Bihar Reports	B.R.
Bihar Revenue and Labour Journal	B.R.L.J.
Bombay Cases Reporter	B.C.R.
Bombay Civil Journal	Bom. C.J.
Bombay High Court Reports	B.H.C.R. or Bom H.C.R.
Bombay Law Reporter	Bom. L.R.
Bombay Printed Judgments	Bom. P.J.
Bombay Rent Cases	Bom. R.C.
Building Law Reports	B.L.R.
Burma Law Journal	Bur. L.J.
Burma Law Reports	Bur. L.R.
Burma Law Times	Bur. L.T.
Calcutta Criminal Law Reports	Cal. Cri. L.R.
Calcutta High Court Notes	Cal. H.C.N.
Calcutta Law Journal	Cal. L.J.
Calcutta Law Reports	Cal. L.R.
Calcutta Law Times	Cal. L.T.
Calcutta Tax Cases	Cal.Tax. C.
Calcutta Weekly Notes (Dacca Reports).	Cal. W.N. (D.R).
Calcutta Weekly Notes	Cal. W.N.
Central India Law Quarterly	C.I.L.Q.
Central Provinces Law Reports	C.P.L.R.
Chandigarh Civil Cases	Ch. C. C.
Chandigarh Criminal Cases	Ch. Cr.C.
Chandigarh Law Reports	Ch. L.R.
Chhattisgarh Law Judgments	Chhat. L.J.
Civil Appeals Judgments (Supreme Court)	Civ. App. J. (SC).

Civil & Military Law Journal	C.M.L.J.
Civil Court Cases	Civ. C.C.
Civil Law Journal	Civ. L.J.
Civil Law Judgments	Civ. L. Jud.
Common Market Law Reports	Com. M.L. Rep.
Common Market Law Review	Com. M.L. Rev.
Company Cases	Comp. Cas.
Company Law Journal	Comp. L.J.
Company News and Reporter	Comp. N.R.
Competition Law Reports	Comp. L.R.
Construction Law Journal	Const. L.J.
Construction Law Reports	Const. L.R.
Consumer Claims Journal	C.C.J.
Consumer Protection Cases	C.P.C.
Consumer Protection Judgments	C.P.J.
Consumer Protection Reporter	C.P.R.
Co-operative Law Journal	Co-op. L.J.
Co-operative Law Reporter	Co-op. L.R.
Co-operative Tribunal Decisions	Co-op. T.D.
Co-operative Tribunal Journal	Co-op. T.J.
Copyright & Trade Marks Reporter	Copy.T.R.
Corporate Law Adviser	Corp. L.A.
Corporate Law Cases	Corp. L.C.
Crimes	Crimes
Criminal Appeals Decision	C.A.D.
Criminal Appeals Reporter	C.A.R.
Criminal Court Judgment	Cri. C.J.
Criminal Law Cases	C.L.C.
Criminal Law Journal (Published by A.I.R)	Cri. L.J.
Criminal Law Reporter (Supreme Court, Gujarat and Maharashtra)	Cri. L.R. (S.C. Guj. & Mah.)
Criminal Law Times	C.L.T.
Current Central Legislation	C.C.L.
Current Civil Cases	Cur. Civ. C
Current Criminal Judgment	Cur. Cri. J.
Current Criminal Reports	C.C.R.
Current Indian Statutes	C.I.S.
Current Labour Reporter	Cur. Lab. R.

Current Law Journal	C.L.J
Current Law Journal (Civil, Criminal & Revenue)	Cur.L.J. (CCR).
Current Legal Reports	Cur. L.R
Current Sales Tax News and Reports	Cur. S.N.R.
Current Service Journal	Cur. Serv. J.
Current Tamil Nadu Cases	C.T.C.
Current Tax Reporter	C.T.R.
Customs Law Manual	C.L.M.
Cuttack Law Times	Cut. L.T.
Cuttack Weekly Reports	Cut. W.R.
Data India	Data India
Delhi Case Law Reporter	Del. C.L.R.
Delhi Law Times	D.L.T.
Delhi Lawyer	Del.L.
Delhi Rent Judgments	D.R.J.
Delhi Reported Judgments	D.Rep.J.
Direct Tax Bulletin	Dir. Tax. Bull.
Divorce and Matrimonial Cases	D.M.C.
Doabia's Election Cases	D.E.
Eastern Criminal Cases	East Cri.C.
Economic & Political Weekly	Eco. & Pol. W.
Education and Service Cases	E.S.C
Education Cases	Ed. Cas
Election Law Reports (Delhi)	E.L. Rs
Environment Law Reports	Env. L.R.
Epitomised Legal Judgments (Labour & Service)	E.L.J. (L&S)
Essential Commodities Cases	E.C.C.
Excise and Customs Cases	Ex. C.C.
Excise and Customs Reporter	Ex. C.R..
Excise and Food Adulteration Reports	Ex. F.R.
Excise Law Times.	Ex. L.T.
Excise Tribunal Reporter	E.T.R.
Exports Imports Times	E.I.T.
Factories Journal Reports	F.J.R
Factories and Labour Reports	Fac. L.R.
Factories and Law Reporter	F.L.R.
Federal Court Reports	F.C.R.

Federal Law Journal	F.L.J.
Food Adulteration Cases	F.A.C.
Food Adulteration Journal	F.A.J.
Foreign Trade Review	F.T. Rev
Gauhati Law Reporter	Gau. L.R.
Gauhati Law Times	Gau. L.T.
Gazette of India	G.O.I.
Gist of Cases (Supreme Court)	G.O.C. (SC)
Goa Law Times	Goa. L.T.
Gujarat Criminal Reports	Guj. Cri. R.
Gujarat High Court Reporter	Guj. H.C.R.
Gujarat Law Herald	Guj. L.H.
Gujarat Law Reporter	Guj. L.R.
Gujarat Law Reports	G.L.R.
Gujarat State Current Statutes	Guj. Sta. Cur. St.
Haryana Rent Reporter	Har. Rent R.
High Court Judgments (Hindi)	H.C.J.
Himachal Law Reporter	Him.L.R.
Hindu Law Reporter	Hin. L.R.
Hyde's Reports	H.R.
Immigration & Nationality Law Reports	Imm. & Nat. L. Rep.
Income Tax Appellate Tribunal Reporter	I.T.A.T.R.
Income Tax Cases	I.T.C.
Income Tax Journal	I.T.J.
Income Tax Reports	I.T.R.
Income Tax Tribunal Cases	I.T.C.
Income Tax Tribunal Decisions	I.T.T.D.
India Quarterly	I.Q.
Indian Cases	Ind. Cas.
Indian Civil Cases.	I.C.C.
Indian Factories and Labour Reports	F.L.R.
Indian Judgment Reporter	Ind. J. Rep.
Indian Judicial Reports	I.J.R.
Indian Jurist	Ind. J.
Indian Law Decisions	Ind. L.D.
Indian Law Reports	I.L.R.
Indian Law Reports (Allahabad)	I.L.R. (All.)
Indian Law Reports (Andhra Pradesh)	I.L.R. (A.P.)
Indian Law Reports (Assam)	I.L.R. (Ass.)

Indian Law Reports (Assam & Nagaland)	I.L.R. (Ass & Naga)
Indian Law Reports (Bombay)	I.L.R. (Bom.)
Indian Law Reports (Calcutta)	I.L.R. (Cal.)
Indian Law Reports (Cuttack)	I.L.R. (Cut.)
Indian Law Reports (Delhi)	I.L.R. (Del.)
Indian Law Reports (Gujarat)	I.L.R. (Guj.)
Indian Factories Journal	I.F.J.
Indian Police Journal	I.P.J.
Indian Rulings	Ind. R.
Indian Tax Cases	Ind. Tax. Cas.
Industrial Court Reporter	I.C.R.
Indian Tax Mirror	I.T.M.
International Law Reporter	Int. L.R
Law Reports, Indian Appeals	Ind. App.
Jabalpur Law Journal	Jab. L.J.
Jaipur Law Reports	Jaipur L.R.
Jammu & Kashmir Law Reports	J.&K. L.R.
Jharkhand Law Journal Reports	Jhar. L.J.R.
Journal of Criminal Cases	JCC
Journal of Shipping, Customs and Transport Laws.	J.S.C.T.L.
Judgement Today	J.T.
Karnataka Law Chronicle	Kant. L.C.
Karnataka Law Journal	Kant. L.J.
Karnataka Legal Decisions	Kant. L.D.
Karnataka Service Law Journal	Kant. Serv.L.J.
Kashmir Law Journal	Kash. L.J.
Kerala High Court & Apex Court Judgments	K.H.C.A.C.J.
Kerala High Court Notes	Ker. H.C.N.
Kerala Law Journal	Ker. L.J.
Kerala Law Journal (Tax Cases)	Ker. L.J. (Tax)
Kerala Law Reporter	Ker. L.R.
Kerala Law Times	Ker. L.T.
Labour and Industrial Cases	Lab. I.C.
Labour Appeal Cases	Lab. A.C.
Labour Law Journal	L.L.J.
Labour Law Notes	L.L.N.
Labour Law Reporter	L.L.R.
Labour Law Times	Lab. L.T.
Lahore Law Times	Lah. L.T.

Land Acquisition & Compensation Cases	L.A.C.C.
(All India) Land Law Reporter	Land L.R.
Land Summary (Andhra Pradesh)	L.S. (A.P.)
Latest Judicial Reports	L.J.R.
Law Reporters (Allahabad)	L.R. (All.)
Law Reports (Mysore)	Law Rep. (Mys.)
Law Reports of India (Supreme Court)	L.R.I. (SC)
Law Reports, Indian Appeals	Ind. App.
Law Summary (Andhra Pradesh)	L.S. (A.P.)
Law Weekly	L.W.
Law Weekly (Criminal)	L.W. (Cri.)
The Lawyer	Law
Legal Surveyor	Legal Surv.
Lower Burma Rulings	Low Bur. R.
Lucknow Law Times	Luck. L.T.
Madhya Bharat Law Journal	Madh. B.L.J.
Madhya Bharat Law Reporter	Madh. B.L.R.
Madhya Bharat	Madh B. or M.B.
Madhya Pradesh Cases	M.P.C.
Madhya Pradesh High Court Today	M.P.H.T.
Madhya Pradesh Law Journal	M.P.L.J.
Madhya Pradesh Law Times	M.P.L.T
Madhya Pradesh Rent Control Journal	M.P.R.C.J.
Madhya Pradesh Weekly Reporter	M.P.W.R.
Madras High Court Reports	Mad. H.C.R.
Madras Law Journal	Mad. L.J.
Madras Law Journal (Criminal)	Mad. L.J. (Cri)
Madras Law Times	Mad. L.Tim.
Madras Law Weekly	M.L.W.
Madras Law Weekly (Criminal)	M.L.W. (Cr)
Madras Weekly Notes	Mad. W.N.
Maharashtra Criminal Reporter	Mah. Cri.R.
Maharashtra Law Journal	Mah. L.J.
(Brahan) Maharashtra Law Reporter	M.L.R.
Maharashtra Rent Control Journal	M.R.C.J.
Marriage Law Journal	Marr L.J.
Marwar Law Reporter	Marwar L.R.
Matrimonial Law Reporter	Mat.L.R.
Mercantile Law Reporter	Mer. L.R.

Moore's Indian Appeals	Moo. Ind. App.
Moore's Privy Council Cases	Moo. P.C.C.
Municipalities and Corporation Cases	Muni & Corpn. C.
Municipal Law Journal	Mun. L.J.
Mysore Chief Court Reporter	Mys. C.C.R.
Mysore High Court Reports	Mys. H.C.R.
Mysore Law Journal	Mys. L.J.
Mysore Law Reports	Mys. L.R.
Nagpur Law Journal	Nag. L.J.
Nagpur Law Reports	Nag. L.R.
North West Provinces High Court Reports	N.W.P.H.C.R.
Official Neutral Citation for Judgments of the Court of Appeal	EWCA
Official Neutral Citation for Judgments of the Court of Appeal (Civil Division)	EWCA (Civ)
Official Neutral Citation for Judgments of the Court of Appeal (Criminal)	EWCA (Crim)
Orissa Criminal Reports	O.C.R.
Orissa Judical Decisions	Ori. J.D.
Orissa Law Review	Ori. L.Rev.
Oudh Cases	Oudh. Cas.
Oudh Law Journal	Oudh. L.J.
Oudh Law Reports	Oudh. L.R.
Oudh Select Cases	Oudh. S.C.
Oudh Weekly Notes	Oudh. W.N.
Patents and Trade Mark Cases	P.T.M.C.
Patent and Trade Mark Reporter	P.T.M.R. Rtr.
Patna Criminal Reports	Pat. Cr.R.
Patna High Court Cases	Pat. H.C.C.
Patna Law Journal Reports	Pat L.J.R.
Patna Law Times	Pat L.Tim.
Patna Law Weekly	Pat L.W.
Patna Weekly Notes	Pat. W.N.
Pepsu Law Reports	Pepsu. L.R.
Prevention of Food Adulteration Journal	P.F.A.J.
Punjab Law Journal	Punj. L. J.
Punjab Law Journal (Criminal)	Punj. L.J. (Cri)
Punjab Law Reporter	Punj. L.R.
Punjab Law Reporter (Delhi)	Punj. L.R. (D)
Punjab Legal Reports and Statutes	Punj. L.R.S.

Punjab Records	Pun. Re.
Punjab Weekly Reporter	Pun. W.R.
Rajasthan Criminal Cases	Raj. Cri.C.
Rajasthan Law Reporter	Rajasthan L.R.
Rajasthan Law Weekly	Ras. L.W.
Rajasthan State Current Statutes	Raj. St. Cur. St.
Rajdhani Law Reporter	Rajdhani L.R.
Rangoon Law Reports	Rang. L.R.
Ratanlal's Unreported Criminal Cases	Rat. Unrep. Cr. C.
Recent Arbitration Judgments	R.Arb.J.
Recent Civil Reports	Rac. Civ. R.
Recent Criminal Reports	Rec. Cr. R.
Recent Laws (Reports)	R.L.
Recent Revenue Reports	R.R.R.
Recent Service Judgments	R.S.J.
Rent Control Journal	R.C.J.
Rent Control Reporter	R.C.R.
Rent Law Reporter	Rent. L.R.
Rent Cases	Rent. Cas.
Revenue Decisions	R.D.
Revenue Law Reporter	Rev. L.R.
Revenue Rulings	Rev. Rul.
Revised Reports	Rev. Rep.
Sales Tax Advices	S.T.A.
Sales Tax Affairs	S.T. Aff.
Sales Tax Cases	S.T.C.
Sales Tax Interpretations	S.T.I.
Sales Tax Literature	S.T.L.
Sales Tax Rulings	S.T.R.
Sales Tax Tribunal Decisions	S.T.T.D.
Saraswati's Privy Council Judgments	Sar.P.C.J.
Saurashtra Law Reporter	Sau. L.R.
Scale (Supreme Court Almanac)	SCALE
Scale (Supreme Court Almanac Short Points)	SCALE S.
SEBI and Corporate Laws	SEBI & C.L
Selected Civil Decisions	S. Civ. Dec.
Service Cases Today	S.C.T.
Services Law Cases	S.L.C.
Service Law Journal	S.L.J.

Service Law Weekly Reporter	S.L.W.R.
Services Law Reporter	S.L.R.
Shome's Law Reports	Shome L.R.
Sikkim Law Journal	Sim. L.J.
Simla Law Cases	Sim. L.C.
Simla Law Journal	Sim. L.J.
Sind Law Reports	Sind. L.R
Speed Post Judgement	S.P.J.
Statutes (Central & T.N.)	Stt. (C & T.N.)
Srinagar Law Journal	Srinagar L.J.
Supreme	Supreme
Supreme Court and Full Bench Rent Cases	S.C.F.B.R.C.
Supreme Court Appeals	S.C.A.
Supreme Court Cases	S.C.C.
Supreme Court Cases (Criminal)	SCC (Cri)
Supreme Court Cases (Labour and Services)	SCC (L&S)
Supreme Court Cases (Supplement)	S.C.C. (Suppl).
Supreme Court Cases (Taxation)	S.C.C. (Tax).
Supreme Court Constitutional Digest	S.C.C.(Digest)
Supreme Court Criminal Rulings	S.C.C. Cr.R.
Supreme Court Decisions	S.C.D.
Supreme Court Journal	S.C.J.
Supreme Court Notes	S.C.N.
Supreme Court Rent Cases	S.C.R.C.
Supreme Court Reports	S.C.R
Supreme Court Sales Tax Judgments	S.C.S.T.J.
Supreme Court Weekly Reports	S.C.W.R.
Supreme Laws Today	S.L.T.
Supreme Reported Judgments	S.R.J.
Supreme Today	Supreme T.
Tamil Nadu Law Notes Journal	T.N.L.N.J.
Tamil Nadu Law Notes Journal (Criminal)	T.N.L.N.J. (Cri).
Tax Affairs	Tax Affairs.
Tax Bar Reporter	Tax. B.R.
Tax Decisions (Supreme Court)	Tax. Dec. (SC)
Tax Gazette	T.G.
Tax Law Review	Tax. L. Rev.
Tax Referencer	Tax. Ref.
Tax Reporter	Tax. Rep.

Tax Saver	Tax. S.
Tax Tribunal Judgments	Tax. Tri.J.
Taxation	Taxation
Taxation Law Reporter	Tax. L.R.
Taxation Law Reports (Notes of Cases)	Tax. L.R. (N.O.C.)
Taxman	Taxman
Transport and Accidents Cases	T.A.C.
Travancore Law Journal	Trav.L.J.
Travancore-Cochin Law Reports	Trav-Co. L.R.
Uchcha Nyayalaya Nirnaya Patrika	Uch. N.P.
United Provinces Law Reports	U.P.L.R.
Unreported Cases (Reporter) (Bombay)	U.C.R. (Bom.)
Unreported Judgments (Supreme Court)	U.J. (SC)
Uttar Pradesh Rent Journal	U.P.R.J
Uttar Pradesh Criminal Cases	U.P. Cri.C.
Uttar Pradesh Criminal Law Cases	U.P. Cri. L.C.
Uttar Pradesh Criminal Law Reports	U.P.Cri.L.R.
Uttar Pradesh Criminal Rulings	U.P.Cri. R.
Uttar Pradesh Law Reports	U.P.L.R.
Uttar Pradesh Law Tribune	U.P.L.T.
Uttar Pradesh Law Tribune (Notes of Cases)	U.P.L.T. (N.O.C).
Uttar Pradesh Local Bodies and Educational Cases	U.P.L.B.E.C.
Uttar Pradesh Rent Control Cases	U.P.R.C.C.
Uttar Pradesh Sales Tax Journal	U.P.S.T.J.
Uttar Pradesh Services Cases	U.P.S.C.
Uttar Pradesh Tax Cases	U.P.T.C.
Uttaranchal Cases	Utt. C.
Vat and Service Tax Cases (Reports)	V.S.T. (Rtr.)
Vat and Service Tax Cases (Statutes)	V.S.T. (St.)
Vikraya Kar Nirnaya	V.K.N.
Vindhya Pradesh	Vind. Pra.
Weekly Law Notes	W.L.N.
Weekly Law Notes (Unreported Cases)	W.L.N. (Unrep. C.)
Weekly Law Reports	W.L.R.
Weir's Criminal Rulings	Weir.
Western Law Cases (Rajasthan)	W.L.C. (Raj).
Western Law Cases (Supreme Court) Civil	W.L.C. (SC, Civ).
Writ Law Reporter	Writ L.R.

APPENDIX II

PERIODICALS AND YEARBOOKS – INDIAN

Name of Periodical or Yearbook	Abbreviation
Academy Law Review	Ac.L.R.
Al Harmony	Al.H.
Aligarh Critical Miscellany	A.C.M.
Amity Law Review	A.L.R.
Amity Law Watch	A.L.W.
Annual Survey of Indian Law	A.S.I.L.
Artha Vijnana	A.V.
Asian Economic Review	A.E.R.
CBI Bulletin	CBI Bull.
Central India Law Quarterly	C.I.L.Q.
Chartered Secretary	C.S.
Cochin University Law Review	C.U.L.R
Contemporary Social Work	C.S.W.
Contribution to Indian Sociology	C.I.S.
Corpus Juris Secundum	C.J.S.
Critical Practice	C.P.
Data Quest	D.Q.
Dr. Ram Manohar Lohia National Law University Journal	R.M.L. N.L.U.J.
Delhi Law Review (Teachers' Edition)	D. L. R. (T.Ed.)
Delhi Law Review (Students' Edition)	D. L. R. (Stud. Ed.)
Economic & Political Weekly	E.P.W
Encounter	Enc.
Foreign Trade Review	F. T. R.
Gandhi Marg	G.M.
Global Religious Vision	G.R.V.
I.C.S.S.R. Journal of Abstracts and Review: Economics	I.C.S.S.R.J.Eco.
I.C.S.S.R. Journal of Abstracts and Review: Sociology	I.C.S.S.R.J.Socio.
India International Centre Quarterly	I.I.C.Q.

Indian Advocate	Ind. Adv.
Indian Archives	I.A.
Indian Association of Social Science Institutions Quarterly	I.A.S.S.I.Q
Indian Bar Review	Ind. Bar. Rev.
Indian Economic and Social History Review	Ind.Eco.Soc.H.Rev.
Indian Economic Journal	I.E.J.
Indian Economic Review	I.E.R.
Indian Journal of Adult Education	I.J.A.E.
Indian Journal of Bio-Chemistry and Bio-Physics	I.J.Biochem.Biophy.
Indian Journal of Biotechnology	I.J.Biotech.
Indian Journal of Chemical Technology	I.J.C.T.
Indian Journal of Chemistry	I.J.Chem.
Indian Journal of Criminology	I.J.Crim.
Indian Journal of Criminology & Criminalistics	Ind. J. Crim. & Crintcs.
Indian Journal of Environmental Law	Ind. J. Env. L.
Indian Journal of Experimental Biology	I.J.Ex.Bio.
Indian Journal of Federal Studies	I.J.F.S
Indian Journal of Information Library and Society	I.J.I.L.S.
Indian Journal of International Law	I.J.I.L.
Indian Journal of Industrial Relations	I.J.I.R.
The Indian Journal of Law and Technology	I.J.L.T.
Indian Journal of Public Administration	I.J.P.A.
Indian Journal of Social Work	I.J.S.W.
Indian Police Journal	I.P.J.
Indian Psychological Abstract & Review	I.Psy.A.Rev.
Indian Socio Legal Journal	I.S.L.J.
International Studies	Int.Stud.
Islamic and Comparative Law Quarterly	Islam. & Comp. L.Q.
Islamic Culture	Islam.Cult.
Jhunjhunu Journal of Legal Education	J.J.L.E.
Journal of Abst & Rev.	J.A. Rev.
Journal of Constitutional and Parliamentary Studies	J. Const. Parl. Stud.
Journal of Indian Law Institute	J.I.L.I.
Journal of Indian School of Political Economy	J.I.S.Pol.E.
Journal of Information and Science	J.L.I.S.
Journal of Intellectual Property Rights	J.I.P.R.
Journal of Legal Studies	J.L.S.

Journal of Objective Studies	J.O.S.
Journal of Parliamentary Information	J.P.I.
Journal of Psychological Research	J.Psy.R.
Journal of Rural Development	J.R.D.
Journal of Scientific and Industrial Research	J.S.I.R.
Journal of the Institute of Human Rights	J.I.Hum.R.
Justitia Osmania University Law Quaterly	J.O.U.L.Q.
Kali's Yug	K.Y.
Kashmir University Law Review	K.U.L.R.
Labour and Development	L.&D.
Law and Justice	Law & Jus.
Law Review	L.R.
Law Teller	L.T.
Lawyers Update	L.U.
The Lawyer's Collective	Law Col.
Legal News and Views	L. News & Views
Maas Journal of Islamic Science	M.J.Islam.Sc.
Madhya Pradesh Journal of Social Sciences	M.P.J.S.S
Maharshi Dayanand University Law Journal	M.D.U.L.J.
Mainstream	Mains.
Management Acknowledgment	Mgmt. Ac.
Management & Change	Mgmt. & Change
Manupatra Intellectual Property Reports	M.I.P.R.
Manushi	Manushi.
March of Law (NLS)	M.O.L. (NLS)
Marg	Marg.
Modern Law Review	Mod. L. Rev.
Nation & the World	N. & W.
National Capital Law Journal	N.C.L.J.
National Law Review	N.L.R.
National Law School Journal	N.L.S.J.
New Law Journal	N.L.J.
Nizam-ul-Quran	N.U.Quran.
NLS Journal	NLS.J.
Nyayadeep	Ny. Dp.
PC Quest	PC.Q.
Perspective in Social Work	Pers.Soc.W.

Popular Jurist	P.J.
Press Council of Indian Review	P.C.I.R.
PRP Journal of Human Rights	P.R.P.J.H.R.
Proceedings of Indian History Congress	Proc.I.H.Cong.
Psychological Studies	Psy.Stud.
Rajasthan Law Weekly	Raj. L.W.
Religion & Law Review	Rel. & L.R.
Research & Development Journal	R. & D.J.
Reserve Bank of India Bulletin	Res.Bank.I.B.
Social Action	S.A.
Social Scientist	S.S.
Social Welfare	S.Wel.
South Asian Economic Journal	S.A.Eco.J.
South Asia Politics	S.A.Pol.
South Asian Studies	S.A.Stud.
Studies in Humanities & Social Science	Stud.Hum.& S.S.
Vidhigyan: The Journal of Legal Awareness	V.J.L.A.
Women's Link	Women. L.
World Affairs	World.A.

APPENDIX III

REPORTERS, PERIODICALS AND YEARBOOKS - INTERNATIONAL

Name of Periodical or Yearbook	Abbreviation
Across Borders	Across Borders
Acta Criminological	Acta Crim.
Acta Juridica	Acta Juri.
Actualites du droit	Actualities
Actualities juridiques, droit administrative	Actualites jur. Dr. admin.
Actualites-Justice	Actualities-justice
Actualite et droit international	Actualite & dr. int.
Actualities de la delegation pour 'Union europeene	Actualites del. U.E.
Actualites d'unidroit	Actualites d'Unidroit
Adelaide Law Review	Adel. L.R.
Adelphia Law Journal	Adelphia. L.J.
Administrative & Regulatory Law News	Admin. & Reg. L.News
Administrative Law Journal of the American University (formerly Administrative Law Journal)	Admin. L.J. Am. U.
Administrative Law Review	Admin. L. Rev.
Advocate	Advocate
Advocate (Idaho)	Advocate(Idaho)
Advocates' Quarterly	Advocates'Q.
Advocates' Society Journal	Advocates' Soc. J.
African-American Law and Policy Report	Afr.-Am.L.& Pol'y Rep.
African Journal of International & Comparative Law	Afr. J.I. & C.
Africa Quarterly	A.Q.
Air Force Law Review	A.F.L. Rev.
Air & Space Law	Air & Space L.
Air & Space Lawyer	Air & Space Law.
Akron Law Review	Akron L. Rev.
Akron Tax Journal	Akron Tax J.

Alabama Law Review	Ala. L. Rev.
Alaska Law Review	Alaska L. Rev.
Albany Law Environmental Outlook	Alb. L. Envtl. Outlook
Albany Law Journal of Science & Technology	Alb. L.J. Sci. & Tech.
Albany Law Review	Alb. L. Rev.
Alberta Law Quarterly	Alta. L. Q.
Alberta Law Review	Alta. L. Rev.
Alberta Reports (1977-)	Alb. R.
Alternatives Journal	Alt. J.
Alpjan Quarterly	Alp. Q.
All England Law Reports	All. E.R.
All England Law Reports Annual Review	All. E.R. Rev.
American Association of Law Libraries Spectrum	A.A.L.L.Spec.
American Bankruptcy Institute Journal	Am. Bankr. Inst. J.
American Bankruptcy Institute Law Review	Am. Bankr. Inst. L. Rev.
American Bankruptcy Law Journal	Am. Bank. L.J.
American Bar Association Antitrust Law Journal	A.B.A. Antitrust L.J.
American Bar Association Criminal Justice	A.B.A. Criminal J.
American Bar Association Entertainment & Sports Lawyer	A.B.A. Enet. & Sports Law.
American Bar Association Family Advocate	A.B.A. Fam. Advocate
American Bar Association Family Law Quarterly	A.B.A. Fam. L.Q.
American Bar Association Journal	A.B.A (Jou.)
American Bar Association Law Practice Management	A.B.A.L.P.M.
American Bar Association Section of Intellectual Property Law	A.B.A.I.P.L.
American Bar Association Tort and Insurance Law Journal	A.B.A. Tort & Ins. L.J.
American Business Law Journal	Am.Bus.L.J.
American Criminal Law Review	Am.Crim.L.Rev.
American Indian Law Review	Am. Indian L. Rev.
American Intellectual Property Law Association Quarterly Journal	A.I.P.L.A.Q.J.
American Journal of Comparative Law	Am.J. Comp. L.
American Journal of Criminal Law	Am.J. Crim.L.
American Journal of International Arbitration	Am.J.Int'l Arb.
American Journal of International Law	A.J.I.L./Am.J.Int'l L.
American Journal of Jurisprudence	Am. J. Juris.
American Journal of Law & Medicine	Am. J.L. & Med.

American Journal of Legal History	Am. J. Legal Hist.
Americian Journal of Tax Policy	Am. J. Tax Pol'y
American Journal of Trial Advocacy	Am. J.Trial Advoc.
American Law and Economics Review	Am. L. & Econ. Rev.
American Law Reports	Am. L.R.
American Review of International Arbitration	Am. Rev. Int'l Arb.
American Society International Law Review	Am. Soc. Int'l L.Rev.
American University International Law Review (Formerly American University Journal of International Law & Policy)	Am. U. Int'l L. Rev.
American Universiy Journal of Gender, Social Policy & the Law (Formerly American Univerisy Journal of Gender & the Law)	Am. U.J. Gender Soc. Pol'y & L.
American University Journal of International Law & Policy	Am. U. J. Int'l L. & Pol'y
American University Law Review	Am. U.L. Rev.
Analyse de politiques	Anal. De pol.
Anglo-American Law Review	Anglo-Am L. Rev.
Animal Law	Animal L.
Annales de droit aerien et spatial	Ann. Air & Sp. L.
Annals of Air and Space Law	Ann. Air & Sp.L.
Annales de droit de Louvain	Ann. Dr. Loub.
Annales de la propriete industrielle, artistique et litteraire	Ann. Pr. Ind. Art & lit.
Annales de l'Universite des sciences socialis de Toulouse	Ann. De l'U.s.s.T.
Annals of Health Law	Annals Health L.
Annuaire canadien des droit international	A.C.D.I.
Annuaire candien de droits desla personne	A.C.D.P.
Annuaire de la Convention europeenne des droits de l'Homme	l'Homme
Annuaire de droit aerien et spatial	Ann. Dr. marit. & aero-spat.
Annuaire de droit maritime et aerien	Ann. Dr. marit. * aer.
Annuaire de droit maritime et aero-spatial	Ann. Dr. marit. & aero-spat.
Annuaire des collectvites locales	Ann. Coll. Loc.
Annuaire francais de droit international	A.F.D.I
Annuaire francais des droits de l'Homme	Ann. Fr. D.H.
Annuaire francais du transport aerien	Ann. Fr. Transp. aer.
Annuaire de la Haye de droit international	Ann. Haye dr. int.

Annuaire de l'Institut de droit international	Ann. Inst.dr. int.
Annuaire international de justice constitutionnelle	Ann. Int. j.c.
Annuaire de là Societe des Nations	Ann. S. N.
Annuaire de la Societe francaise de droit aerien et spatial	Ann. S. fr. Dr. aer. & spat.
Annuaire de legislation etrangere	Ann. Leg. Etrang.
Annuaire de legislation francaise	Ann. Leg. Fr.
Annuaire de philosophie de droit	Ann. Phil. Dr.
Annuaire des Nations Unies	An. N.U.
Annuaire Suisse de droit international	Ann. Suisse dr. int.
Annual Review of Banking Law	Ann. Rev. Banking L.
Annual Survey of American Law	Ann. Surv. Am. L.
Annual Survey of Australian law	Ann. Surv. Austl. L.
Annual Survey of Commonwealth Law	Ann. Surv. Commonwealth L.
Annual Survey of English Law	Ann. Surv. Engl. L.
Annual Survey of International & Comparative Law	Ann. Surv. Int'l & Comp.L.
Annual Survey of South African Law	Ann. Surv. S.Afr. L.
Antitrust	Antitrust
Antitrust Bulletin	Antitrust Bull.
Antitrust Law and Economics Review	Antitrust L.& Econ. Rev.
Antitrust Law Journal	Antitrust L.J.
Anuario Mexicano de Derecho International	An . Mex. Der. Int'l
Appeal: Review of Current Law and Law Reform	Appeal
Arab Law Quarterly	Arab L.Q.
Arbitration International	Arb. Int'l
Archiv des Olfentlichen Rechts	A.O.R.
Archiv fur di civilistische praxis	A.C.P.
Archiv fur rechts und Sozialphilosophie	A.R.S.P.
Archivum Juridicum Cracoviense	Arch. Jur. Cracoviense
Arizona bar Jounal	Ariz.Bar. J.
Arizona Journal of International & Comparative Law	Ariz. J. Int'l & Comp. L.
Arizona Law Review	Ariz. L. Rev.
Arizona State Law Journal	Ariz. St. L.J.
Arkansas Law review	Ark. L. Rev.
Art, Antiquity, and the Law	Art. Ant. & L.
Artificial Intelligence and Law	A.I. & L.
Army Lawyer	Army Law.

Asia Law Review	Asia L. R.
Asian Law Journal	Asian L.J.
Asia Pacific Journal of Environmental Law	Asia Pac. J. Envtl. L.
Asia-Pacific Journal of Human Rights and the Law	Asia Pac. J.H.R. & L.
Asia-Pacific Journal of International Law	Asia Pac.J. int'l. L.
Asia-Pacific Law Review	Asia Pac. L. Rev.
Asian-Pacific American Law Journal (formerly Asian American Pacific Islands law Journal)	Asian Pac. Am. L.J.
Asian-Pacific Law & Policy Journal	Asian Pac. L. & Pol'y J.
Atlantic Reporter (USA)	A.
Atomic Energy Law Journal	A.E.L.J.
Auckland University Law Review	Auckland U.L. Rev.
Australian & New Zealand Journal of Criminology	Austl. Crim. & N.Z.J.
Australian Bar Review	Austl. Bar Rev.
Australian Business Law Review	Austl. Bus. L. Rev.
Australian Competition and Consumer Law Journal	Austl. Comp. & Cons. L.J.
Australian Insurance Law Journal	Austl. Ins. L.J.
Australian Journal of Contract Law	Austl.J. Contract L.
Australian Journal of Family Law	Austl. J. Fam. L.
Australian Journal of Human Rights	Austl. J. H.R.
Australian Journal of Labour Law	Austl. J. Lab. L.
Australian Journal of Legal History	Austl. J. L.H.
Australian Law Journal	A.L.J.
Australian Law Journal Reports	A.L.J.R.
Australian Legal Monthly Digest	A.L.M.D.
Australian Property Law Journal	Austl. Prop. L.J.
Australian Tax Review	Aus. T. Rev.
Australian Torts Law Journal	Aust. Torts L.J.
Austrian Journal of Public and International law	Aus.J. Pub. & Int'l L.
Austrian Review of International and Europe Law	Aus. Rev. Int'l & Eur. L.
Baltimore Law Review	Bal. L.R.
Banking And Finance Law Review	B.F.L.R.
Banking Law Journal	Banking L.J.
Banking Policy Report	Banking Pol'y Rep.
Bankruptcy Developments Journal	Bankr. Dev. J.
Banque et droit	B.& dr.
Bar & Bench News Digest	Bar & Bench N.D.

Baylor Law Review	Baylor L. Rev.
Barrister	Barrister
Behavioural Sciences and the Law	Behav. Sci. & L.
Berkeley Journal of Employment and Labour law	Berkeley J. Emp. & Lab. L.
Berkeley Journal of Health Care Law	Berkeley J. Health Care L.
Berkeley Journal of International Law	Berkeley J. Intl. L.
Berkeley Technology Law Journal	Berkeley Tech. L.J.
Berkeley Women's Law Journal	Berkeley Women's L.J.
Biotechnology Law Report	Biotech. L. Rep.
Boletin Mexicano de Derecho Comparado	Bol. Mex. Der. Comp.
Bollettino dell Instituto di diritto romano	Boll. Inst. dir. rom.
Bond Law Review	Bon. L.R.
Boston Bar Journal	Boston Bar J.
Boston College Enviromental Affairs Law Review	B.C. Envtl. Aff. L. Rev.
Boston College International & Comparative Law Review	B.C. Int'l. & Comp. L. Rev.
Boston College Law Review	B.C.L. Rev.
Boston College Third World Law Journal	B.C. Third World L.J.
Boston University International Law Journal	B.U.Int'l. L.J.
Boston University Journal of Science & Technology Law	B.U.J. Sci & Tech L.
Boston University Journal of Tax Law	B.U.J. Tax L.
Boston University Law Review	B.U.L.Rev
Boston University Public Interest Law Journal	B.U. Pub. Int. L.J.
Brandeis Law Journal	Brandeis L.J.
Briefly Speaking	Brief. Speaking
Brigham Young University Law Review	B.Y.U.L. Rev.
British Columbia Law Notes	B.C.L.N.
British Columbia Law Reports	B.C.L.R.
British Company Law Cases	B.C.L.C.
British Institute of International and Comparative Law	Brit. Inst. Int'l & Comp. L.
British Journal of Criminology	Brit.J.Crim.
British Tax Review	Brit. Tax Rev.
British Yearbook of International Law	Brit. Y.B. Int'l L.
Brooklyn Law Review	Brook. L. Rev.
Buffalo Enviromental Law Journal	Buff. Envtl. L.J.
Buffalo Human Rights Law Review	Buff. H.R.L. Rev.
Buffalo Law Review	Buff.L.Rev.

Buffalo Public Interest Law Journal	Buff. Pub. Int. L.J.
Buffalo Women's Law Journal	Buff. Women's L.J.
Bulletin Canadien VIH-SIDA et droit	Bull Can. VIH-SIDA & D.
Bulletin of Legal Developments	Bull. Leg. Dev.
Bulletin d'information sur les activites Juridiques (Conseil de I'Europe)	Bull. Info act. Jur.
Bureau of National Affairs Patent, Trademark and Copyright Journal	B.N.A. Patent, T.M. & Copyright J.
Business and the Law	Bus. & L.
Business Law Review	Bus. L. Rev.
Business Law	Bus. L.
Business Lawyer	Bus. Law.
Business Quarterly	Busi. Qua.
Cahiers de droit	C. de D.
Cahiers de droit de l'entreprise	C. de D. entr.
Cahiers de Droit europeen	C. de D. eur.
Cahiers du Conseil Constitutionnel	C. du Cons. Const.
Cahiers de I'Instiut quebecois d'administration judiciaire	C.I.Q.A.J.
California Bankruptcy Journal	C.B.J. or Cal. Bankr. J.
California Criminal Law Review	Cal. Crim. L. Rev.
California Regulatory Law Reporter	Cal. Reg. L. Rep.
California State Bar Journal	Cal. St. B.J.
California Western International Law Journal	Cal. W. Int'l L.J.
California Western Law Review	Cal. W.L. Rev.
Cambridge Law Journal	Cambridge L.J.
Cambridge Yearbook of European Legal Studies	Cambridge Y.B. Eur. Legal Stud.
Campbell Law Review	Campbell L. Rev.
Canada Law Journal	Can. L.J.
Canada-United States Law Journal	Can.-U.S.L.J.
Canadian Bar Association Papers	C.B.A.P.
Canadian Bar Journal	Can. Bar. J.
Canadian Bar Review	Can. Bar Rev.
Canadian Bioethics Report	Can. Bioethics R.
Canadian Business Law Journal	Can. Bus. L.J.
Canadian Business Review	Can. Bus. Rev.
Canadian Class Action Review	Can. Class Action Rev.

Canadian Communications Law Review	Can. Comm. L. Rev.
Canadian Community Law Journal	Can. Community L.J.
Canadian Competition Policy Record	Can. Compet. Pol'y Rec.
Canadian Competition Record	Can. Comp. Rec.
Canadian Council on International Law:Proceedings	Can. Council Int'l L. Proc.
Canadian Criminal Law Review	Can. Crim L. Rev.
Canadian Criminology Forum	Can. Crim. Forum
Canadian Current Tax	Can. Curr. Tax
Canadian Environmental Law News	Can. Envtl. L.N.
Canadian Family Law Quarterly	Can. Fam. L.Q.
Canadian HIV/AIDS Policy & Law Review	Can. HIV/AIDS Pol'y & Rev.
Canadian Human Rights Advocate	Can. H.R. Advoc.
Canadian Human Rights Yearbook	Can. Hum. Rts. Y.B
Canadian Intellectual Property Review	C.I.P.R.
Canadian International Lawyer	Can. Int'l Law.
Canadian Journal of Administrative Law & Practice	Can. J. Admin. L. & Prac.
Canadian Journal of Corrections	Can. J. Corr.
Canadian Journal of Criminology	Can. J. Crim.
Canadian Journal of Criminology and Corrections	Can. J. Crim. & Corr.
Canadian Journal of Family Law	Can. J. Fam.L.
Canadian Journal of Insurance Law	Can. J. Ins. L.
Canadian Journal of International Business Law and Policy	Can. J. Int'l Bus. L. & Pol'y
Canadian Journal of Law and Jurisprudence	Can. J.L. & Jur.
Canadian Journal of Law and Society	C.J.L.S.
Canadian Journal of Law and Technology	C.J.L.T.
Canadian Journal of Women and the Law	C.J.W.L.
Canadian Labour & Employment Law Journal	C.L.E.L.J.
Canadian Law Libraries	Can.L.L.
Canadian Law Review	Can. L. Rev.
Canadian Law Times	Can. L.T.
Canadian Lawyer	Can. Law.
Canadian Legal Studies	Can. Legal Stud.
Canadian Municipal Journal	Can. Mun. J.
Canadian Native Law Bulletin	Can. N.L.Bull.
Canadian Public Policy	Can. Pub. Pol'y
Canadian Tax Foundation (Conference Report/ Rapport de conference)	Can. Tax Found.

Canadian Tax Highlights	Can. Tax Highlights
Canadian Tax Journal	Can. Tax J.
Canadian Tax News	Can. Tax N.
Canadian Taxation:A Journal of Tax Policy	Can. Tax'n:J.Tax Pol'y
Canadian Yearbook of International Law	Can. Y.B. Int'l Law
Canberra Law Review	Canb. L. Rev.
Capital University Law Review	Capital U.L. Rev.
Cardozo Arts & Entertainment Law Journal	Cardozo Arts & Ent. L.J.
Cardozo Electronic Law Bulletin	Cardozo E.L. Bull.
Cardozo Journal of International & Comparative Law (Formerly New Europe Law Review)	Cardozo J. Int'l & Comp.L.
Cardozo Law Review	Cardozo L. Rev.
Cardozo Studies in Law and Literature	Cardozo Stud. L. & Lit.
Cardozo Women's Law Journal	Cardozo Women's L.J.
Caribbean Law Review	Caribbean L. Rev.
Carolina Law Journal	Car. L.J.
Case Western Reserve Journal of International Law	Case W. Res. J. Int'l L.
Case Western Reserve Law Review	Case. W, Res. L. Rev.
Catholic Lawyer	Cath. Law.
Catholic University Review	Cath. U. Rev.
Chapman Law Review	Chapman L. Rev.
Chicago Journal of International Law	Chicago J. Int'l L.
Chicago-Kent Law Review	Chicago-Kent L. Rev.
Chicago Lawyer	Chicago Law.
Chicago Legal Forum	Chicago Legal F.
Chicano-Latino Law Review (formerly Chicano Law Review)	Chicano-Latino L. Rev.
Children's Legal Rights Journal	Child. Legal Rts. J.
China Law Reporter	China L. Rep.
Chinese Yearbook of International Law and Affairs	Chinese Y.B. Int'l & Aff.
Chitty's Law Journal	Chitty's L.J.
Circles: Buffalo Women's Journal of Law & Social Policy	Circles
Civil Liberties Review	Civ. Lib. Rev.
Civil Justice Quarterly	C.J.Q.
Cleveland State Law Review	Clev. St. L. Rev.
Cleveland-Marshall Law Review	Clev. Marshall L. Rev.
Clinical Law Review	Clinical L. Rev.

Coastal Management	Coastal Mgmt.
Codicillus	Codicillus
Colorado Journal of International Environmental Law & Policy	Colo. J. Int'l E.L. & Pol'y
Colorado Lawyer	Colo. Law.
Columbia Business Law Review	Colum. Bus. L. Rev.
Columbia Human Rights Law Review	Colum. H.R.L. Rev.
Columbia Journal of Asian Law (formerly Journal of Chinese Law)	Colum. J. Asian Law
Columbia Journal of East European Law	Colum. J. E. Eur. L.
Columbia Journal of Environmental Law	Colum. J. Envtl. L.
Columbia Journal of European Law	Colum. J. Eur. L.
Columbia Journal of Gender and Law	Colum. J. Gender & L.
Columbia Journal of Law and Social Problems	Colum. J.L. & Soc. Probs.
Columbia Journal of Transnational Law	Colum. J. Transnat'I L.
Columbia Law Review	Colum. L. Rev.
Columbia Science and Technology Law Review	Colum. Sci. & Tech. L. Rev.
Columbia –V.L.A. Journal of Law & the Arts	Colum. – V.L.A.J.L. & Arts.
Commercial Law Journal	Com. L.J.
Commercial Leasing Law and Strategy	Com. Leasing L. & Strategy
Common Law World Review	C.L. World Rev.
Common Market Law Review	C.M.L. Rev.
Commonwealth Human Rights Law Digest	Commonwealth H.R.L.D.
Communication & the Law	Comm. & L.
Commonwealth Law Bulletin	Commonwealth L. Bull.
Commonwealth Legal Education	Commonwealth Legal Educ.
Communication Law & Policy	Comm. L. & Pol'y
Communications Lawyer	Comm.. Law.
Communique/International Court of Justice	Communique I.C.J.
Comparative and International Law Journal of Southern Africa	Comp. & Int'l L.J.S. Afr.
Comparative Juridical Review	Comp. Jurid. Rev.
Comparative Labour Law & Policy Journal *(formerly Comparative Labour Law Journal) (formerly cited as Comp. Lab. L.J.)*	Comp. Lab. L. & Pol'y J.
Comptes rendus stenographiques des debats (Conseil de I'Europe)	Debat

Computer Law and Security Report	Computer L. & Sec. R.
Computer Law Review and Technology Journal	Computer L. Rev. & T.J.
Computer Lawyer	Computer Law.
Congressional Digest	Cong. Dig.
Connecticut Bar Journal	Conn. B.J.
Connecticut Insurance Law Journal	Conn. Ins. L.J.
Connecticut Journal of International Law	Conn. J. Int'l L.
Connecticut Law Review	Conn. L. Rev.
Connecticut Probate Law Journal	Conn. Prob. L.J.
Constitutional Commentary	Const. Commentary
Constitutional Forum Constitutionnel	Const. Forum Const.
Constitutional Review	Const. Rev.
Consumer Finance Law Quarterly Report	Cons. Fin. L.Q. Rep.
Construction Law Journal	Construction L.J.
Construction Lawyer	Construction Law.
Continuity and Change	Continuity & Change
Copyright Bulletin	Copyright Bull.
Cooley Law Review	Cooley L. Rev.
Cornell International Law Journal	Cornell Int'l L.J.
Cornell Journal of Law & Public Policy	Cornell J.L. & Pub. Pol'y
Cornell Law Review	Cornell L. R.
Cornell Law Journal	Cornell L.J.
Corporate Management Tax Conference	Corp. Mgmt. Tax Conf.
Corporate Taxation	Corp. Tax'n
Corpus Juris Secundum	C.J.S.
Correspondences Judiciaries	Corr. Jud.
Counsellor: The New York Law School Journal	Counsellor
Cours de perfectionnement du notariat	C.P. du N.
Creighton Law Review	Creighton L. Rev.
Crime, Law and Social Change	Crime, L. & Soc. Change
Criminal Law Forum	Crim. L.F.
Criminal Law Quarterly	Crim L.Q.
Criminal Law Review	Crim. L. Rev.
Criminology	Criminol. or Criminal.
Critical Criminology	Crit. Criminol.
Croatian Arbitration Yearbook	Crotain Arb. Y.B.
Croatian Critical Law Review	Croat. Crit. L. Rev.

Crown Counsel's Review	Crown Coun. Rev.
Cumberland Law Review	Cumb. L. Rev.
Current Law Yearbook	Curr. L.Y.B.
Current Legal Problems	Curr. Legal Probs.
Current Medicine for Attorneys	Current Med. For Att'ys
Currents: International Trade Law Journal	Currents
Cyberspace Law Journal	Cyberspace L.J.
Cyberspace Lawyer	Cyberspace Law.
Dalhousie Journal of Legal Studies	Dal. J. Leg. Stud.
Dalhousie Law Journal	Dal. L.J.
Defense Counsel Journal	Def. Couns. J.
Delaware Journal of Corporate Law	Del. J. Corp. L.
Delaware Law Review	Del. L. Rev.
Delaware Lawyer	Del. Law.
Denver Journal of International Law & Policy	Denv J. Int'l L. & Pol'y
Denever University Law Review (*formerly Denver Law Journal)*	Denv. U.L. Rev.
Department of State Bulletin	Dep't St. Bull.
DePaul Business Law Journal	DePaul Bus. L.J.
DePaul International Law Journal	DePaul Int'l L.J.
DePaul Journal of Health Care Law	DePaul J. Health Care L.
DePaul Law Review	DePaul L. Rev.
DePaul-L.C.A. Journal of Art and Entertainment Law and Policy	DePaul-L.C.A. Art & Ent. L. & Pol'y
Deutsche Richterzeitung	D. RiZ.
Deutsches and Europaisches Familienrecht	D.E.F.R.
Dickinson Journal of Environmental Law & Policy	Dick. J. Envtl. & Pol'y
Dickinson Journal of International Law	Dick. J. Int'I L.
Dickinson Law Review	Dick. L. Rev.
Digital Technology Law Journal	D.T.L.J.
Dispute Resolution Journal (*formerly Arbitration Journal)*	Disp. Resol. J.
District of Columbia Law Review	D.C.L. Rev.
Documents juridiques internationaux	D.J.I.
Documents (Working Papers) (Council of Europe)	Documents
Documents de séance (Conseil de I'Europe)	Documents
Drake Journal of Agricultural Law	Drake J. Agric. L.
Drake Law Review	Drake L. Rev.

Droit Aftician du Travail	D.A.T.
Droit des societies	Dr. societies
Droit et cultures	Dr. et Cult.
Droit et patrimoine	Dr. Et. Pat.
Droit et pratique du commerce international	D.P.C.I.
Droit et Societe	Dr. et. Soc.
Droit europeen des transports	Dr eur. Transp.
Droit Maritime Francias	Dr. Marit. Fr.
Droit Japonais contemporain	Dr Japon. Contemp.
Droit Social	Dr. soc.
Droits	Droits
Duke Environmental Law & Policy Forum	DEL
Duke Journal of Comparative & International Law	Duke J. Comp. & Int'l L.
Duke Journal of Gender Law & Policy	Duke J. Gender L. & Pol'y
Duke Law Journal	Duke L.J.
Duke Law and Technology Review	Duke L. & Tech. Rev.
Duquense Business Law Journal	Duq. Bus. L.J.
Duquesne Law Review	Duq.L. Rev.
East European Business Law	E. Eur. Bus. L.
East European Constitutional Review	E. Eur. C. Rev.
Ecology Law Quarterly	Ecology L.Q.
Edinburg Law Review	Ed. L. Rev.
Educational & Law Journal	Educ. & L.J.
Elder Law Journal	Elder L.J.
Election Law Journal	Election L.J.
Electronic Journal of Comparative Law	E.J.C.L.
Emory International Law Review (*formerly Emory Journal of International Dispute Resolution*)	Emory Int'l L. Rev.
Emory Law Journal	Emory L.J.
Employee Rights & Employment Policy Journal	Employee Rts. & Employment Pol'y J.
Energy Law Journal	Energy L.J.
English Reports	E.R.
Entertainment & Media Law Reports	Ent. M. L.R.
Entertainment & Sports Lawyer	Ent. & Sports Law.
Entertainment Law & Finance	Ent. L. & Fin.
Environmental Law	Envtl. L.

Entertainment Law Review	Ent. L.R.
Environmental Law and Management	Envtl. L. & Mgmt.
Environmental Law and Policy Journal	Envtl. L. & Pol'y J.
Environmental Law Journal	Envtl. L.J.
Environmental Lawyer	Envtl. Law.
Environmental Policy and Law	Envtl. Pol'y & L.
Environmentally Friendly: The Journal of the Pace Center for Environmental Legal Studies	Envtlly. Friendly
Environs Environmental Law and Policy Journal	Environs Envtl. L.& Pol'y J.
Estates and Trusts Journal	E. & T.J.
Estates and Trusts Quarterly	E. & T.Q.
Estates Trusts & Pensions Journal	E.T.P.J.
Ethics	Ethics
Europarecht	EuR.
Europaische Zeitschrift fur Privatrecht	E.Z.P.R.
European Access	Eur. Access
European Business Law Review	Eur. Bus. L.Rev.
European Competition Law Review	Eur. Comp. L. Rev.
European Environmental Law Review	Eur. Envtl. L. Rev.
European Environment Yearbook	Eur. Env. Y. B.
European Human Rights Law Review	Eur. H.R.L. Rev.
European Intellectual Property Review	Eur. I.P. Rev.
European Journal of Criminal Policy & Research	Eur. J. Crim. Pol'y & Research
European Journal for Education Law and Policy	Eur. J. Educ. L. & Pol'y
European Journal of Health Law	Eur. J. Health L.
European Journal of International Law	E.J.I.L.
European Journal of Law & Economics	Eur. J.L.& Econ.
European Journal of Law & Reform	Eur. J.L. Ref.
European Journal of Migration and Law	Eur. J. Migr. & L.
European Journal of Crime, Criminal Law and Criminal Justice	Eur. J. Crime, Crim. L. & Crim. J.
European Law Journal	Eur. L.J.
European Law Quarterly	Eur. L.Q.
European Law Review	Eur. L. Rev.
European Legal Forum	Eur. Leg. F.
Eruopean Review of Private Law	E.R.P.L.

European Trade Mark Reports	Eur. T.M.R.
European Transport Law	Eur. Transp. L.
Examiner	Examiner
F.A.A. Aviation New	F.A.A. Av. N.
Family Court Reporter	Fam. Ct. R.
Family Court Review (formerly Family & Conciliation Courts Review)	Fam. Ct. Rev.
Family Law Quarterly	Fam. L.Q.
Family Law Review	Fam. L. Rev.
Federal Bar News & Journal	Fed. B. News & J.
Federal Circuit Bar Journal	Fed. Circuit B.J.
Federal Communications Law Journal	Fed. Comm. L.J.
Federal Courts Law Review	Fed. Cts.'L. Rev.
Federal Lawyer	Fed. Law.
Federal Litigator	Fed. Litigator
Federal Reporter (USA)	Fed. R.
Federal Rules Decisions	F.R.D.
Federal Supplement (USA)	Fed. Sup.
Femi-Juris: Current Cases	Femi-Juris: C.C.
Feminist Legal Studies	Fem. Legal Stud.
Financial Law Reports	Fin. L.R.
Fleet Street Reports	F.S.R.
Florida Bar Journal	Flo. B.J.
Florida Coastal Law Journal	Flo. Coastal L.J.
Florida International Law Journal	Flo. Int'l L.J.
Florida Law Review (formerly University of Florida law Review)	Flo. L. Rev.
Florida State Journal of Transnational Law & Policy	Flo. St. J. Transant'l L. & Pol'y
Florida State University Journal of Land Use & Environmental Law	Flo. St. U.J. Land Use & Envtl. L.
Florida State University Law Review	Flo. St. U. L. Rev.
Florida Tax Review	Flo. Tax Rev.
Food & Drug Law Journal	Food & Drug L. J.
Fordham Environmental Law Journal	Fordham Envtl. L. J.
Fordham Finance, Securities & Tax Law Forum	Fordham Fin. Sec. & Tax L. F.
Fordham Intellectual Property, Media & Entertainment Law Journal	Fordham I.P. Media & Ent. L.J.

Fordham Journal of Corporate and Finance Law	Fordham J. Corp. & Fin. L.
Fordham Law Review	Fordham L. Rev.
Fordham Urban Law Journal	Fordham Urb. L. J.
Froncesis: Revista	Froncesis
International Law FORUM du droit international	FORUM
George Mason Law Review (formely George Mason University Law Review and George Mason Independent Law Review)	Geo. Mason L. Rev.
George Mason University Civil Rights Law Journal	Geo. Mason U. Civ. Rts. L.J.
George Washington International Law Review (formely George Washington Journal of International Law and Economics)	Geo. Wash. Int'l L. Rev.
George Washington Law Review	Geo. Wash. L. Rev.
Georgetown Immigration law Journal	Geo. Immigr. L.J.
Georgetown International Environmental Law Review	Geo. Int'l Envtl. L. Rev.
Georgetown Journal of Gender and the Law	Geo. J. Gender & L.
Georgetown Journal of International Law	Geo.J.Int'l L.
Georgetown Journal of Legal Ethics	Geo. J. Legal Ethics
Georgetown Journal on Poverty Law & Policy & *(formerly Georgetown Journal on Fighting Poverty)*	Geo. J. on Poverty L. Pol'y
Georgetown Law Journal	Geo L.J.
Georgetown Public Policy Review	Geo. Pub. Pol'y Rev.
Georgia Journal of International and Comparative Law	Ga. J. Int'l & Comp.L.
Georgia Law Review	Ga. L. Rev.
Georgia State University Law Review	Ga. St. U.L. Rev.
Global Journal on Crime and Criminal Law	Global J. On Crime & Crime. L.
Global Law Review	Global L. Rev.
Golden Gate University Law Review	Golden Gate U.L. Rev.
Gonzaga Law Review	Gonz. L. Rev.
Great Plains Natural Resources Journal	Great Plains Nat. Resources J.
Green Law: Journal of the Pace Environmental Law Program(*formerly Environmentally Friendly*)	Greenlaw
Green's Weekly Digest	G.W.D.
Griffith Law Review	Griffith L.R.
Hague Yearbook of International Law	Hague Y. B. Int'1 L.
Hamline Journal of Public Law and Policy	Hamline J.Pub. L.& Pol'y

Hamline Law Review	Hamline L. Rev.
Harvard BlackLetter Law Journal	Harv. BlackLetter L.J.
Harvard Civil Rights-Civil Liberties Law Review	Harv. C.R. C.L.L.Rev.
Harvard Environmental Law Review	Harv. Envtl. L. Rev.
Harvard Human Rights Journal (*formerly Harvard Human Rights Yearbook*)	Harv. Hum. Rts. J.
Harvard International Law Journal	Harv. Int'l L.J.
Harvard Journal of Law and Gender	Harv. J. L. & Gender
Harvard Journal of Law and Public Policy	Harv. J.L. & Pub. Pol'y
Harvard Journal of Law and Technology	Harv. J. L. & Tech.
Harvard Journal on Legislation	Harv. J. on Legis.
Harvard Law Review	Harv. L. Rev.
Harvard Negotiation Law Review	Harv. Negot. L. Rev.
Harvard Women's Law Journal	Harv. Women's L. J.
Hastings Communications & Entertainment Law Journal	Hastings Comm. & Ent. L.J.
Hastings Constitutional Law Quarterly	Hastings const. L. Q.
Hastings International and Comparative Law Review	Hastings Int'l & Comp. L. Rev.
Hastings Law Journal	Hastings L.J.
Hastings West-Northwest Journal of Environmental Law and Policy	Hastings W-Nw. J. Envtl. L. & Pol'y
Hastings Women's Law Journal	Hastings Women's L.J.
Hawaii Bar Journal	Haw. B.J.
Hawaill Law Review	Haw. L. Rev.
Health and Human Rights	Health & Hum. Rts.
Health Law in Canada	Health L. Can.
Health Law Journal	Health L.J.
Health Lawyer	Health Law.
Health Matrix	Health Matrix
Heidelberg Journal of International law	Heidelberg J. Int'l L.
High Technology Law Journal	High Tech. L. J.
Hitotsubashi Journal of Law and Politics	H.J.L.P.
Hofstra Law Review	Hofstra L. Rev.
Hofstra Property Law Journal	Hofstra Prop. L. J.
Holdsworth Law Review	Hold L. R.
Hong Kong Law Journal	Hong Kong L.J.
Housing Law Reports	H.L.R.

Houston Journal of International Law	Hous. J. Int'l L.
Houston Law Review	Hous. L. Rev.
Howard Law Journal	How. L. J.
Howard Scroll: The Social Justice law Review	How. Scroll.
Human Rights Internet Reporter	H.R.I.R.
Human Rights Law Journal	H.R.L.J.
Human Rights Case Digest	Hum. Rts. Case Digest
Human Rights in Development	Hum. Rts. Dev.
Human Rights in Developing Countries	Hum. Rts. Dev. Countries
Human Rights Journal	Hum. Rts. J.
Human Rights Quarterly	Hum. Rts. Q.
Human Rights Tribune	Hum. Rts. Trib.
Humboldt Forum Recht	Humboldt F.R.
ICSID Review	ICSID Rev.
Idaho Law Review	Idaho L. Rev.
IDEA: The Journal of Law and Technology	IDEA
ITC Quarterly	I.T.C.Q.
Illinois Bar Journal	Ill. B.J.
Illinois Law Quarterly	Ill. L.Q.
ILSA Journal of International & Comparative Law	ILSA J. Int'l & Comp. L.
Immigration Appeals Report	Immigr. App. R.
Immigration & Nationality Law & Practice	Immigr. & Nat'lity L. & P.
Immigration and Nationality Law Review	Immigr. & Nat'lity L. Rev.
IMPACT Labour law & Management Practices	IMPACT
Index to Legal Periodicals & Books	I.L.P. & B.
Indiana International and Comparative Law Review	Ind. Int'l & Comp. L. Rev.
Indiana Journal of Global Legal Studies	Ind. J. Global Legal Stud.
Indiana Law Journal	Ind. L.J.
Indiana Law Review	Ind. L. Rev.
Indigenous Law Journal	Indigenous L.J.
Industrial Law Journal	Indus. L.J.
Industrial Relations Law Journal	Indus. Rel. L.J.
Industrial Relations Law Reporters	Ind. Rel. L.R.
Industrial Relations Legal Information Bulletin	Ind. Rel. L. Rel. Bull.
Industrial & Labour Relations Reviews	Indus. & Lab. Rel. Rev.
Information Bulletin on Legal Affairs	Inf. Bull. L.A.
Information Bulletin on Legal Affairs (Council of Europe)	Inf. Bull.

Information and Communications Technology Law	I.& Comm. T.L.
Insolvency Law & Practice	Ins. L. & P.
Insolvency Bulletin	Ins. Bull.
Institute of Advanced Legal Studies Bulletin	I.A.L.S. Bull.
Intellectual Property Journal	I.P.J.
Intellectual Property Law Bulletin	I.P.L.Bull.
Intellectual Property Newsletter	I.P.L. Newsl.
Intellectual Property Quarterly	I.P.Q.
Intellectual Property & Technology Law Review	I.P. & T.L.R.
International and Comparative Law Quarterly	Int'l & Comp. L. Q.
International Arbitration Law Review	Int'l Arb. L. Rev.
International Business Law Journal	I.B.L.J.
International Business Lawyer	Int'l Bus. Law.
International Commercial Litigation	Int'l Com. Lit.
International Commission of Jurists Review	Int'l Comm. Jur. Rev.
International Company and Commercial Law Review	Int'l Co. & Com. L. Rev.
International Comparative Corporate Law Journal	Int'l Comp. Corp. L.J.
International and Comparative Law Quarterly	I.C.L.Q.
International Comparative Law Review	Int'l Comp. L. Rev.
International Criminal Law Review	Int'l. Crim. L. Rev.
International Financial Law Review	Int'l Fin. L. Rev.
International Insights	Int'l Insights
International Insurance Law Review	Int'l Ins. L. Rev.
International Journal	Int'l J.
International Journal for the Semiotics of Law	Int'l J. Sem. L.
International Journal of Children's Rights	Int's J. Child. Rts.
Internatiional Journal of Communications Law & Policy	Int'l J. Comm. L. & Pol'y
International Journal of Comparative Law & Industrial Relations	Int. J. Comp. L.L.I.R.
International Journal of Comparative Labour law and Industrial Relations	Int'l J. Comp. lab. L. & Ind. Rel.
Internatioinal Journal of Conflict Management	Int'l J. Confl. Mgmt.
International Journal of Estuarine and Coastal Law	Int. J. Est. & C.L.
I-CON International Journal of Constitutional Law	I.J.C.L.
International Journal of Cultural Property	Int'l J. Cult. Prop.
International Journal of Franchising and Distribution Law	Int'l J. Franch. & Distrib. L.
International Journal of Human Rights	Int'l J.H.R.
International Journal of Law Policy and the Family	Int'l J.L. Pol'y & Fam.

International Journal of Law and Information Technology	Int'l J.L. & I.T.
International Journal of Law and psychiatry	Int'l J.L. & Psychiatry
International Journal of Legal Information	Int'l J. Legal Info.
International Journal of Offender Therapy and Comparative Criminology	Int'l J. Off Ther. & Comp. Crim.
International Journal of Refugee Law	Int'l J. Refugee. L.
International Journal of the Sociology of Law	Int'l Soc. L.
International Labour Review	Int. Lab. Rev.
International Lawyer	Int'l Law.
International Legal Materials	I.L.M.
International Legal Perspectives	Int'l Legal Persp.
International Legal Practitioner	Int'l Leg. Practitioner
International Legal Theory	Int'l L. Theory
International Maritime and Commercial Law Yearbook	Int'l Mar. & Com. L.Y.B.
International Media Law	Int. Med. L.
International Review of Administrative Science	Int. Rev. Ad. Sc.
International Review of Criminal Policy	Int'l Rev. Crim. Pol'y
International Review of Industrial Property and Copyright Law	Int'l Rev. Ind. Prop & C' right L.
International Review of Law Computers & Technology	Int'l Rev. L. Comp. & Tech.
International Review of Law & Economics	Int'l Rev. L. & Econ.
International Review of Red Cross	Int'l Rev. Red Cross
International Tax and Business Lawyer	Int'l Tax & Bus. Law.
International Trade Law and Practice	Int'l Trade L. & Pract.
International Trade Law & Regulation	Int'l Trade L. Reg.
International Trade law Quarterly	I.T.L.Q.
International Trust & Estate Law Reports	Int. T. & E.L.R.
Interrights Bulletin	I.Bull.
Iowa Law Review	Iowa L. Rev.
Irish Jurist	Ir. Jur.
Irish Law Reports Monthly	Ir. L.R.M.
Irish Law Times	Ir. L.T.
Islamic Law & Society	Islamic L. & Soc.
Israel Law Review	Isr. L.R.
Issues in Law & Medicine	Issues L. & Med.
ITU News	ITU N.
Jahrbuch fur recht und ethic	J.B.R.E.

Jersey Law Review	J.L. Rev.
Jewish Law Report	Jewish L. R.
John Marshall Journal of Computer & Information Law	J. Marshall J. Computer & Info. L.
John Marshall Law Quarterly	J. Marshall L.Q.
John Marshall Law Review	J. Marshall L. Rev.
Journal des juges provinciaux	J.J. Prov.
Journal des Tribunaux	J. Tribunaux
Journal Des Tribunaux-Droit Europeen	J. Tribun. Droit Eur.
Journal du Barreau	J. Barreau
Journal du droit des jeunes	J. dr. jeunes
Journal du droit international	J.D.I.
Journal of Affordable Housing & Community	J. Aff. Housing & Community
Development Law	Dev. L.
Journal of African Law	J. Afr. L.
Journal of Agricultural Law	J. Agric. L.
Journal of Air Law	J. Air L.
Journal of Air law and Commerce	J. Air. L & Com.
Journal Of Appellate Practice & Process	J. App. Pr. & Pro.
Journal of Art & Entertainment Law	J. Art & Ent. L.
Journal of Bio Law & Business	J. BioLaw & Bus.
Journal of Business Law	J. Bus. L.
Journal of Catholic Legal Studies	J. Cath. Legal Stud.
Journal of Child Law	J. Child. L.
Journal of Chinese Law	J. Chinese. L.
Journal of College & University Law	J. C. & U.L.
Journal of Common Market Studies	J.Com. Mkt. S.
Journal of Commonwealth Law and Legal Education	J. Commonwealth L. & Legal Educ.
Journal of Comparative Business and Capital Market Law	J. Comp. Bus. & Cap. Mkt. L.
Journal of Conflict and Security Law	J. Confl. & Sec. L.
Journal of Conflict Resolution	J. Confl. Resolution
Journal of Constitutional Law in Eastern and Central Europe	J. Const. L. E. & Cent. Eur.
Journal of Contemporary Health Law & Policy	J. Contemp. Health L. & Pol'y

Journal of Contemporary Law	J. Contemp. L.
Journal of Contemporary Legal Issues	J. Contemp. Legal Issues
Journal of Contract Law	J.Cont. L.
Journal of Corporate Taxation	J. Corp. Tax'n
Journal of Corporation Law	J. Corp. L.
Journal of Criminal Justice Education	J. Crim. J. Educ.
Journal of Criminal Law	J. Crim L.
Journal of Criminal Law & Criminology	J. Crim. L. & Criminology
Journal of Dispute Resolution	J. Disp. Resol.
Journal of Energy Law & Policy	J. Energy L. & Pol'y
Journal of Energy, Natural Resources & Environmental Law	J. Energy, Nat'l Res. & Envtl. L.
Journal of Environmental Law	J. Envtl. L.
Journal of Environmental Law & Litigation	J. Envtl. L. & Litig.
Journal of Environmental Law & Practice	J. Envtl. L & Prac.
Journal of European Integration	J. Eur. Int.
Journal of Family Law	J. Fam. L.
Journal of Gender, Race & Justice	J. Gender Race & J.
Journal of Health and Hospital Law	J. Health & Hosp. L.
Journal of Health Care Law & Policy	J. health Care L. & Pol'y
Journal of Health Politics, Policy & Law	J. Health Pol. Poly. L.
Journal of the History of International Law	J. Hist. Int'l L.
Journal of the Indian Law Institute	J.I.L.I.
Journal of Information, Law and Technology	J.I.L.T.
Journal of Institute for Human Rights	J.I.H.R.
Journal of Integrated Bar of the Philippines	J.Inte.Bar. Phil.
Journal of the Institute for the Study of Legal Ethics	J.I.S.L.E.
Journal of Intellectual Property	J. Intell. Prop.
Journal of Intellectual Property Law	J. Intell. Prop. L.
Journal of International Property Law	J. Intell. Prop. L.
Journal of International Arbitration	J. Int'l Arb.
Journal of International Banking Law	J.I.B.L.
Journal of International Economic Law	J. Int'l Econ. L.
Journal of International Financial Markets	J. Int'l. Fin. Markets
Journal of International Franchising & Distribution Law	J. Int'l Fran. & Dist. L.
Journal of International Law & Business	J. Int'l & Bus.
Journal of International Legal Studies	J. Int'l Legal Stud.

Journal of International Taxation	J. Int'l Tax
Journal of International Wildlife Law and Policy	J. Int'l Wildlife L. & Pol'y
Journal of Internet Law	J. Internet. L.
Journal of Juvenile Law	J. Junvenile L.
Journal of Land use & Environmental Law	J. Land Use & Envtl. L.
Journal of Land, Resources & Environmental Law *(formerly Journal of Energy, Natural Resources & Environmental Law)*	J. Land Resources & Envtl. L.
Journal of Law & Commerce	J. L. & Com.
Journal of Law & Economics	J. L. & Econ.
Journal of Law, Economics & Organization	J. L. Econ. & Org.
Journal of Law & Education	J. L. & Educ.
Journal of Law and Environment	J. L. & Env't
Journal of Law and Equality	J.L. & Equality
Journal of Law & Family Studies	J.L. & Fam. Stud.
Journal of Law & Health	J.L. & Health
Journal of Law & Information Science	J.L. & Infor. Sci.
Journal of Law & Policy	J.L. & Pol'y
Journal of Law & Politics	J.L. & Pol.
Journal of Law & Religion	J.L. & Religion
Journal of Law and Social Policy	J.L. & Soc. Pol'y
Journal of Law and Society	J.L. & Soc'y
Journal of Law in Society	J.L. in Soc'y
Journal of Law, Medicine & Ethics	J.L. Med. & Ethics
Journal of Law & Technology	J.L. & Tech.
Journal of Legal Advocacy & Practice	J. Legal Advoc. & Prac.
Journal of Legal Economics	J. Legal Econ.
Journal of Legal Education	J. Legal Educ.
Journal of Legal History	J. Legal Hist.
Journal of Legal Medicine	J. Legal Med.
Journal of Legal Pluralism	J. Legal Pluralism
Journal of Legal Studies	J. Legal Stud.
Journal of Legislation	J. Legis.
Journal of Legislation & Public Policy	J. Legis, & Pub. Pol'y
Journal of Leningard University	J. Leningard. U.
Journal of Malaysian & Comparative Law	J. Mal. & Comp. L.
Journal of Maritime Law & Commerce	J. Mar L. & Com.

Journal of Media Law & Practice	J. Med. L. & P.
Journal of Medicine and Law	J. Med & L.
Journal of Mineral Law & Policy	J. Min. L. & Pol'y
Journal of Multistate Taxation	J. Multistate Tax'n
Journal of Natural Resources & Environmental Law *(formerly Journal of Mineral Law & Policy)*	J. Nat. Resouces & Envtl. L.
Journal of Partnership Taxation	J. Partnership Tax'n
Journal of Personal Injury Litigation	J. Pers. Inj. Lit.
Journal of Pharmacy & Law	J. Pharmacy & L.
Journal of Planning & Environmental Law	J. Plan. & Envtl. L.
Journal of Private International Law	J. P. Int'l L.
Journal of Products Liability	J. Prod. Liab.
Journal of Proprietary Rights	J. Proprietary Rts.
Journal of Science & Technology Law	J. Sci. & Tech. L.
Journal of Small & Emerging Business Law	J.Small & Emerging Bus. L.
Journal of Social Welfare Law	J. Soc. Welfare L.
Journal of Social Welfare and Family Law	J. Soc. Welfare & Fam. L.
Journal of South Pacific Law	J. S. Pac. L.
Journal of Southern Legal History	J. S. Legal Hist.
Journal of Space Law	J. Space L.
Journal of Taxation	J. Tax'n
Journal of Technology Law & Policy	J. Tech. L. & Pol'y
Journal of the Institute for the Study of Legal Ethics	J. Inst. for Study of Legal Ethics
Journal of the Law Society of Scotland	J.L.S.S.
Journal of the Legal Profession	J. Legal Prof.
Journal of the Patent & Trademark Office Society	J. Pat. & Trademark Off. Soc'y
Journal of the Suffolk Academy of Law	J.Suffolk Academy L.
Journal of Transnational Law & Policy	J. Transnat'l L. & Pol'y
Journal of World Intellectual Property	J. World. I. P.
Journal of World Trade	J. World Trade
Journal of World & Trade Law, Economics and Policy	J. World Trade L. Econ. & Pol'y
Journal Officiel des Communautes europeennes: Communication s et Information	J.O.C.
Journal Official des Communautes europeennes: Debats du parlement europeen	J.O.D.

Journal Official des Communautes europeenes Legislation	J.O.L.
Judicature	Judicature
Juridical Review	Jurid. Rev.
Justice of Peace Journal	J.P.J.
Juvenile and Family Court Journal	Juv. & Fam. C.J.
Kanas Journal of Law & Public Policy	Kan. J.L. & Pub. Pol'y
Kanas Law Review	Kan. L. Rev.
Kentucky Children's Rights Journal	Ky. Children's Rts. J.
Kentucky Law Journal	Ky. L.J.
Kentucky Law Review	Ky. L. Rev.
Kings College Law Journal	Kings C. L.J.
Kingstan Law Review	Kingstan L.R.
Korean Journal of Air and Space Law	Korean J. Air & Sp. L.
Korean Journal of Comparative Law	Korean J. Comp. L.
Korean Journal of International and Comparative Law	Korean J. Int'l & Comp. L.
La Raza Law Journal	La Raza L.J.
Labour Law Journal	Lab. L.J.
Labour Lawyer	Lab. Law.
Land and Water Law Review	Land & Water L. Rev.
Law & Contemporary Problems	Law & Contemp. Probs.
Law & Inequality	Law & Inequality
Law & Justice	Law & Jus.
Law and History Review	L.H.R.
Law and Philosophy	Law & Phil.
Law and Philosophy : an International Journal for Jurisprudence and Legal Philosophy	Law & Phil. Int'l J.
Law & Policy	Law & Pol'y
Law & Policy in International Business	Law & Pol'y Int'l Bus.
Law and Politics Book Review	Law & Pol. Book Rev.
Law & Practice of International Courts & Tribunals	Law & Prac. Int'l Courts & Trib.
Law & Psychology Review	Law & Psychol. Rev.
Law & Sexualty : A Review of Lesbian & Gay Legal issues	Law & Sexuality
Law & Social Inquiry	Law & Soc. Inquiry
Law & Society Review	Law & Soc'y Rev.
Law Department Management	Law Dep't Mgmt
Law Firm Partnership & Benefits Report	Law Firm Partnership & Ben. Rep.

Law Librarian	Law. Librn.
Law Library Journal	Law Libr. J.
Law Office Management & Administration Report	Law Off. Mgmt & Admin. Rep.
Law Office Technology Review	Law Off. Tech. Rev.
Law Practice Management *(formerly Legal Economics)*	Law Prac. Mgmt.
Law Quarterly Review	Law Q. Rev.
Law Reports of the Commonwealth	L.R.C.
Law Review of Michigan State University Detroit College of Law	Law Rev. Mich. St. U. Det. C.L.
Law Society Gazette (Law Society of Upper Canada)	L. Soc'y Gaz. & Guardian Gaz.
Law Technology and Insurance	Law Tech. & Ins.
Law, Text, Culture	Law Text Culture
Law Times	L.T.
Lawyers Journal *(formerly Pittsburg Legal Journal)*	Pittsburgh Legal J.
Legal History Review	Legal Hist. Rev.
Legal Information Management	Legal Info. Mgmt.
Legal Issues of Economic/European Integration	L.I.E.I.
Legal Medical Quarterly	L. Med. Q.
Legal Reference Services Quarterly	Leal Ref. Serv. Q.
Legal Studies	Legal Stud.
Legal Theory	Legal Theory
Leiden Journal of International Law	Leiden J. Int'l L.
Lewis and Clerk Law School Environmental Law	E.N.V.T.L.
Lex Electronic : Revue du droit des technologies de I' information	Lex Electronica
Liverpool Law Review	Liverpool. L.R.
Lyod's Maritime and Commercial Law Quarterly	L.M.C.L.Q.
Local Courts' and Municipal Gazette (Toronto)	Local Ct. Gaz.
Los Angeles Lawyer	L.A. Law
Louisiana Bar Journal	La. B.J.
Louisiana Law Review	La L. Rev.
Lower Canada Jurist	L.C. Jurist
Lower Canada Law Journal	L.C.L.J.
Loyola Consumer Protection Journal	Loy. Con. Prot. J.
Loyola Law Review (New Orleans)	Loy. L. Rev.
Loyola of Los Angeles Entertainment Law Journal	Loy. L.A. Ent. L.J.

Loyola of Los Angeles International & Comparative Law Journal	Loy. L.A. Int'l Com. L.J.
Loyola of Los Angeles Law Review	Loy. L.A. L. Rev.
Loyola Poverty Law Journal	Loy Poverty L.J.
Loyola University of Chicago Law Journal	Loy. U. Chicago L.J.
Lyods Maritime & Commercial Law Quarterly	Lyods M. & C.L.Q.
Maastricht Journal of European and Comparative Law	M.J.E.C.L.
Macquarie Journal of International and Comparative Environmental Law	Macq. J. Int'l & C. Envtl. L.
Maine Law Review	Me. L. Rev.
Malaya Law Review	Mal. L. Rev.
Malayan Law Journal	M.L.J.
Malaysian Journal of Law & Society	Mal. J.L. & S.
Manitoba Bar News	Man. Bar N.
Manitoba Law Journal	Man. L.J.
Manx Law Bulletin	Manx. L. Bull.
Maori Law Review	Maori L. Rev.
Marquette Intellectual Property Law Review	Marq. Intell. Prop. L. Rev.
Marquette Law Review	Marq. L. Rev.
Marquette Sports Law Review	Marq. Sports L. Rev.
Maryland Journal of Contemporary Legal Issues	Md J. Contemp. Legal Issues
Maryland Journal of International Law and Trade	Md. J. Int'l L. & Trade
Maryland Law Review	Md. L. Rev.
Massachuetts Law Review	Mass. L. Rev.
Massachusetts Legal History	Mass. L. His.
McGeorge Law Review *(formerly Pacific Law Journal)*	McGeorge L. Rev.
McGill International Journal of Sustainable Development Law and Policy	McGill Int'l J.S. D.L.P.
McGill Law Journal	McGill L.J.
Media Law & Policy	Media L. & Pol'y
Medicine, Science and the Law	Med. Sci. Law
Medical Law Review	Med. L. Rev.
Medicine & Law	Med. & L.
Medico-Legal Journal	Med. Leg. J.
Melbourne University Law Review	Melbourne U.L. Rev.
Meloncsian Law Journal	Mel. L.J.
Mercer Law Review	Mercer L. Rev.

Mexico Trade & Law Reporter	Mex. Trade & L. Rep.
Michigan Bar Journal	Mich. B.J.
Michigan Business Law Journal	Mich. Bus. L.J.
Michigan Journal of Gender & Law	Mich. J. Gender & L.
Michigan Journal of International Law	Mich. J. Int'l L.
Michigan Journal of Law Reform	Mich. J.L. Reform
Michigan Journal of Race & Law	Mich. J. Race & L.
Michigan Law Review	Mich. L. R.
Michigan Law & Policy Review	Mich. L. & Pol'y Rev.
Michigan Law Journal	Mich. L.J.
Michigan Law Review	Mich. L. Rev.
Michigan State University – D.C.L. Journal of International Law	MSU-DCL.J. Int'l. L
Michigan Telecommunications & Technology Law Review	Mich. Telecomm. & Tech. L. Rev.
Military Law Review	Mil. L. Rev.
Minnesota Intellectual Property Review	Minn. Intell. Prop. Rev.
Minnesota Journal of Global Trade	Minn. J. Global Trade
Minnesota Law Review	Minn. L. Rev.
Mississippi College Law Review	Miss. C.L. Rev.
Mississippi Law Journal	Miss. L.J.
Mississippi Law Review	Miss. L. Rev.
Missouri Environmental Law & Policy Review	Mo. Envtl. L. & Pol'y Rev.
Missouri Law Review	Mo. L. Rev.
Monash University Law Review	Monash U.L. Rev.
Monde Juridique	Monde Jur.
Money Laundering Law Report	Money Laundering L. Rep.
Montana Law Review	Mont. L. Rev.
Motana Lawyer	Mont. Law
Monthly Labour Review	Monthly Lab. Rev.
Murdoch University Electronic Journal of Law	Murdoch U.E.J.L.
NAFTA: Law & Business Review of the Americas	NAFTA L. & Bus. Rev. Am.
National Banking Law Review	Nat'l Banking L. Rev.
National Black Law Journal	Nat'L Black L.J.
National Insolvency Review	Nat'l Insolv. Rev.
National Institute of Justice Journal	Nat'l Inst. Just. J.
National Journal of Constitutional Law	N.J.C.L.

National Journal of Sexual Orientation Law	Nat'l J. Sexual Orientation. L.
National Law Journal	Nat'l L.J.
National Law Review	Nat'l L. Rev.
National Real Property Law Review	Nat'l Real P.L.R.
National Tax Journal	Nat'l Tax J.
Natural Resources & Environment	Nat. Resource & Env't
Natural Resources Journal	Nat. Resources J.
Naval Law Review	Nav. L. Rev.
Nebraska Law Review	Neb. L. Rev.
Neptunus: Martime and Oceanic Law Review	Neptunus
Netherlands International Law Review	Nethl. Int'l L. Rev.
Netherlands Quarterly of Human Rights	Nethl. Q.H.R.
New England International and Comparative Law Annual	New Eng. Int'l & Comp. L. Ann.
New England Journal of Medicine	New Eng. J. Med.
New England Journal on Criminal & Civil Confinement	New Eng. J. on Crim. & Civ. Confinement
New England Law Review	New Eng. L. Rev.
New Europe Law Review	New Eur. L. Rev.
New jersey Lawyer	N.J. Law.
New Law Journal	New L.J.
New Mexico Law Review	N.M.L. Rev.
New York City Law Review	N.Y. City L. Rev.
New York International Law Review	N.Y. Int'l L. Rev.
New York Law Journal	N.Y.L.J.
New York Law Review	N.Y.L. Rev.
New York Law School Journal of Human Rights	N.Y.L Sch. J. Hum. Rts.
New York Law School Journal of International & Comparative Law	N.Y.L. Sch. J. Int'l & Comp. L.
New York Law School Law Review	N.Y.L. Sch. L. Rev.
New York State Bar Journal	N.Y. St. B.J.
New York Supplement	N.Y.S.
New York University Clinical Law Review	N.Y.U. Clin. L. Rev.
New York University East European Constitutional Review	N.Y.U. E. Eur. Const. Rev.
New York University Environmental Law Journal	N.Y.U. Envtl. L.J.
New York University International Journal of Constitutional Law	N.Y.U. Int'l J. Cont. L.

New York University Journal of International Law & Policy	N.Y.U.J. Int'l & Pol.
New York University Law Review	N.Y.U.L. Rev.
New York University Review of Law & Social Change	N.Y.U. Rev. l. & Soc. Change.
New Zealand Company Law Cases	N.Z. Comp. L.C.
New Zealand Law Journal	N.Z.L.J.
New Zealand Law Reports	N.Z.L. Rep.
New Zealand Law Review	N.Z.L. Rev.
New Zealand Universities Law Review	N.Z.U.L. Rev.
NEXUS: A Journal of Opinion	NEXUS: J. Opinion
Nigerian Law Journal	Nig. L.J.
Non-Profit Law Yearbook	Non-Profit L. Yearbook
Non-State Actors and International Law	Non-State Act. & Int'l L.
Nordic Journal of International Law	Nordic J. Int'l L.
North Carolina Central Law Journal	N.C. Centr. L.J.
North Carolina Journal of International Law & Commercial Regulation	N.C.J. Int'l L & Com. Reg.
North Carolina Law Review	N.C.L. Rev.
North Dakota Law Review	N.D.L. Rev.
Northern Illinois University Law Review	N. Ill. U.L. Rev.
Northern Ireland Legal Quarterly	N. Ir. Legal Q.
Northern Kentucky Law Review	N.Ky. L. Rev.
Northwestern Journal of International Law & Business	Nw. J. Int'l L & Bus.
Northwestern University Law Review	Nw. U.L. Rev
Notaries International	Notaries Int'l
Notre Dame International Law Review	Notre Dame Int'l L. Rev.
Notre Dame Journal of Law Ethics & Public Policy	Notre Dame J.L. Ethics & Pub. Pol'y
Notre Dame Law Review	Notre Dame L. Rev.
Nova Law Review	Nova L. Rev.
Nuclear Law	Nuclear L.
Ocean & Coastal Law Journal *(formerly Territorial Sea Journal)*	Ocean & Coastal L.J.
Ocean Development & International Law	Ocean Devel. & Int'l L.
OECD Journal of Competition Law and Policy	OECD J. Comp. L. & Pol'y
Official Journal of European Communities	O.J.
Official Journal of the European Communities Debates of the European Parliament	O.J. Deb.

Official Journal of the European Communities: English Special Edition	O.J. Sp. Ed. Eng.
Official Journal of the European Communities: Information and Notices	O.J.I.. & N.
Official Journal of the European Communities: Legislation	O.J.L.
Official Report of Debates (Council of Europe)	Debates (Council of Europe)
Ohio Northern University Law Review	Ohio N.U.L. Rev.
Ohio State Journal on Dispute Resolution	Ohio St. J. Disp. Resol.
Ohio State Law Journal	Ohio St. L.J.
Oil and Gas Law and Taxation Review	Oil & Gas. L. & T. Rev.
Oklahoma City University Law Review	Okla. City U.L. Rev.
Oklahoma Law Review	Okla. L. Rev.
Ombudsman Journal	Ombudsman J.
Ontario Family Law Bulletin	Ont. Fam. L. Bull.
Ontario Lawyers Gazette	Ont. Law. Gaz.
Ontario Securities Commission Bulletin	O.S.C. Bull.
Orders of the Day and Minutes of Proceedings (Council of Europe)	Orders
Orders du jour et process-verbaux (Counseil de I'Europe)	Orders
Oregon Law Review	Or. L. Rev.
Osaka University Law Review	Osaka U.L. Rev.
Osgoode Hall Law Journal	Osgoode Hall L.J.
Osteuropa-Recht	Osteuropa.-R.
Otago Law Review	Otago L. Rev.
Ottawa Law Review	Ottawa L. Rev.
Oxford Journal of Legal Studies	Oxford J. Legal Stud.
Oxford University Commonwealth Law Journal	O.U.C.L.J.
Pace Environmental Law Review	Pace Envtl. L. Rev.
Pace International Review *(formerly Pace Yearbook of International Law)*	Pace Int'l Rev.
Pace Law Review	Pace L. Rev.
Pacific Law Journal	Pac. L.J.
Pacific Rim Law & Policy Journal	Pac. Rim L. & Pol'y J.
Palmer's Company Cases	Palmer C.C.
Panstwo I Prawo	Panstwo I Prawo
Patient Law Annual	Pat. L. Ann.
Penn State Law Review	Penn. St. L. Rev.

Pepperding Law Review	Pepp. L. Rev.
The Philanthropist	Philanthropist
Philippine Law Journal	Philippine L.J.
Pittsburgh Legal Journal	Pittsburg Legal J.
Planning Law Reports	Pl. L.R.
Police Journal	Police J.
Polish Contemporary Law.	Polish Contemp. L.
Polish Yearbook of International Law	Polish Y.B. Int'l L.
Potomac Law Review	Potomac L. Rev.,
Prison Service Journal	Prison Serv. J.
Probate & Property	Prob. & Prop.
Probate Law Journal	Prob. L.J.
Probation Journal	Prob. J.
Procurement Lawyer	Procurement Law.
Products Liability Law Journal	Prod. Liab. L.J.
Provinicial Judges Journal	Prov. Judges J.
Psychology, Public Policy & Law	Psycho. Pub. Pol'y & L.
Public Contract Law Journal	Pub. Cont. L.J.
Public Interest Law Review	Pub. Int. L. Rev.
Public Land Law Review	Pub. Land L. Rev.
Public Land & Resources Law Review	Pub. Land & Resources L. Rev.
Public Law	Pub. L.
QLR *(formerly Bridgeport Law Review)*	QLR
Queen's Law Journal	Queen's L.J.
Quinnipiac Health Law Review	Quinnipiac H.L. Rev.
Quinnipiac Probate Law Journal *(formerly Connecticut Probate Law Journal)*	Quinnipiac Prob. L.J.
Ration Juris	Ration Juris
Real Estate Law Journal	Real Est. L.J.
Real Estate Law Report	Real Est. L. Rep.
Real Property, Probate & Trust Journal	Real Prop. Prob.& Tr. J.
Recueil des Cours	Rec. des Cours
Reforms	Reforms
Regant University Law Review	Regent U.L. Rev.
Relations Industrielles	R.I.

Res Communes: Vermont's Journal of the Environment	Res Communes: Vermont's J.
Environment	Env't
Response Meridiana	Response Merid
Responsabilite civile et assurances	Resp. civ. Et assur.
Restitution Law Review	R.L.R.
Review of Central and East European Law	Rev. Cent. & E. Eur. L.
Review of Constitutional Studies	Rev. Const. Stud.
Review of European Community and International Environmental Law	R.E.C.I.E.L.
Review of Litigation	Rev. Litig
Revista Europea De Derecho de la Navegacion Maritima Y Aeuronautica	R.E.D.N. M.A.
Revista Juridica de la Universidad Interamliricana De Puerto Rico	Rev. Jur. U.I.P.R.
Revista Juridica Universidad de Puerto Rico	Rev. Jur. U.P.R.
Revista Romania De Drept.	Rev. Rom. Dr.
Revue Administrative	Rev. Admin.
Revue africaine de droit international et compare	R.A.D.I.C.
Revue algerienne des sciences juridiques, economiques et Politiques	Rev. A.S.J.E.P.
Revue belge de droit constitutionnel	Rev. B.D. Const.
Revue belge de droit international	Rev. B.D.I.
Revue canadienne de criminolie	Rev. can. crim
Revue canadienne de droit communautaire	Rev. can. Dr. commun.
Revue canadienne de droit de commerce	Rev. can. Dr. comm..
Revue candienne de Droit Familial	Rev. can. Dr. Fam.
Revue canadienne de droit international	R.C.D.I.
Revue canadienne droit et societe	R.C.D.S.
Revue Canadienne de propriete intellectuelle	R.C.P.I.
Revue candiene du droit d' auteur	R.C.D.A.
Revue critique	Rev. Crit.
Revue critique de droti international prive	Rev. crit. Dr. int. prive
Revue critique de jurisprudene belge	R.C.J.B.
Revue critique de legislation et de jurisprudence du Canada	R.C.L.J.
Revue de la common law en francais	R.C.L.F.
Revue de droit de I'ULB	Rev. Dr. ULB

Revue de droit d'Ottawa	R.D. Ottawa
Revue de droit de l'Universite de Sherbrooke	R.D.U.S.
Revue de droit de l'Universite du Nouveau-Brunswick	R.D.U.N.-B.
Revue de droit de McGill	R.D. McGill.
Revue de droit des affaires internationales	R.D.A.I.
Revue de droit immobilier	R.D. Imm.
Revue de droit international de science diplomatiques et politiques	R.D.I.S.D.P
Revue de droit social	R.D.S.
Revue de droit uniforme	Rev. D.U.
Revue de jurisprudence	R. De j.
Revue de l'arbitrage	Rev. arb.
Revue de legislation et de jurisprudence	R. de L.J.
Revue de planification fiscale et successorale	R.P.F.S.
Revue du Barreau	R. du. B.
Revue du Barreau canadien	R. du B. can.
Revue d'etudes constitutionnelles	R. etudes const.
Revue d'etudes juridiques	R.E.J.
Revue d'histoire du droit	Rev. hist. dr.
Revue d'historie du droit international	Rev. hist. dr. int.
Revue d'integration europeenne	R.I.E.
Revue due droit	R. du D.
Revue du droit de l'union europeenee	R. du D.
Revenue du droit de l'union europeenne	R.D.U.E.
Revue dudroit public et de la science politique en France et a l'etranger	Rev. D.P. & S.P.
Revue du Notariat	R. du N.
Revue de la recherché juridique	R.R.J.
Revue de planfication fiscaleet successorale	R.P.F.S.
Revue des droits de thomme (Human Rights Journal)	H.R.J.
Revue des Juristes de l'ontario	Rev. jurists de l'ont.
Revue des societies	Rev. societies
Revue egyptienne de droit international	Rev. E.D.I.
Revue europeenee de droit prive	R.E.D. Prive
Revue europeenne de droit public	R.E.D. Public
Reveue europeenne de philosophie et droit	R.E.P.D.
Revue Femmes et Droit	R.F.D.

Revue Francaise De Droit Administratif	Rev. fr. Dr. admin.
Revue Francaise de droit aerien et spatial	Rev. fr. Dr. aerien
Revue Francaise de droit constitutionnel	Rev. fr. Dr. constl.
Revue generale de droit	R.G.D.
Revue generale de droit international Public	R.G.D.I.P.
Revue generale du droit des assurances	R.G.D.A.
Revue hellenique de droit international	R.H.D.I.
Revue historique de droit francais et etranger	Rev. hist. dr. fr. & etran.
Revue Interdisciplinaire d' etudes juridiques	Rev. Interdiscipl. Et. Jur.
Revue international de droit compare	Rev. Inter. Dr. Comp.
Revue international de droit economique	R.I.D. Econ.
Revue international de droit penal	Rev. I.D.P.
Revue internationale de droit et politique de development durable de McGill	R.D.P.D.D. McGill
Revue Internationale de la Croix-Rouge	R.I.C.R.
Revue internationale de la propriete indusrielle et artistique	R.I.P.I.A.
Revue internationale de politique Criminelle	Rev. I.P.C.
Revue Internationale du droit d'auteur	R.I.D.A.
Revue internationale de Semiotique Juridique	R.I.S.J.
Revue Juridique de I'environement	R.J.E.
Revue juridique des etudiants et etudiantes de I'universite Laval	R.J.E.U.L.
Revue juridique La femme et le droit	Rev. jur. Femme dr.
Revue juridique themis	R.J.T.
Revue nationale de droit constitutionnel	R.N.D.C.
Revue quebecoise de droit international	R.Q.D.I.
Revue sui sse de droit international et de droit europeen	R.S.D.I.E.
Revue Suisse de jurisprudence	R.S.J.
Revue trimestrielle de droit civil	R.T.D. civ.
Revue trimestrielle de droit commercial et de droit economique	Rev. trim. Dr. com.
Revue trimestrille de droit europeen	R.T.D. eur.
Revue universelle des droits de I'homme	R.U.D.H.
Richmond Journal of Global Law & Business	Rich. J. Global L. & Bus.
Richmond Journal of Law & Technology	Rich. J.L. & Tech.
Richmond Journal of Law and the Public Interest	Rich. J.L. & Int.
Rivista di Diritto Internazionale	R.D.I.

Roger Williams University Law Review	Roger Williams U.L. Rev.
Roma e America. Diritto Romano Commune	Dir. Rom. Com.
Rutgers Computer & Technology Law Journal	Rutgers Computer & Tech. L.J.
Rutgers-Camden Law Journal	Rutgers – Camden L.J.
Rutgers Journal of Law and Religion	Rutgers J.L. & Religion
Rutgers Law Journal	Rutgers L.J.
Rutgers Law Review	Rutgers L. Rev.
Rutgers Race and the Law Review	Rutgers Race & L. Rev.
Saint John's Journal of Legal Commentary	St. John's J. Legal Comment.
Saint John's Law Review	St. John's L. Rev.
Saint Louis University Law Journal	Saint Louis U.L.J.
Saint Louis University Public Law Review	St. Louis U. Pub. L. Rev.
Saint Louis-Warsaw Transatlantic Law Journal	St. Louis – Warsaw Transatlantic L.J.
Saint Mary's Law Journal	St. Mary's L.J.
Saint Thomas Law Review	St. Thomas L. Rev.
San Diego Law Review	San Diego L. Rev.
San Joaquin Agricultural Law Review	San Joaquin Agric. L. Rev.
Santa Clara Computer & High Technology Law Journal	Santa Clara Computer & High Tech. L.J.
Santa Clara Law Review	Santa Clara L. Rev.
Saskatchewan Bar Review	Sask. Bar Rev.
Saskatchewan Law Review	Sask. L. Rev.
Scandinavian Studies in Law	Scan. Stud. L.
Scottish Current Law Year Book	Scot. Curr. L.Y.B.
Schweizerische Juristen-Zeitung	S.J.Z.
Schweizerische Zeitschriff fur internationals und Europaischen Recht	S.Z.I.E.R.
Scottish Law Gazette	Scott. L.G.
Scottish Law Times	Scott. L.T.
Scottish Planning Law & Practice	Scoth. Pl. L. & P.
Seattle University Law Review (*formerly University of Puget Sound Law Review)*	Seattle U.L. Rev.
Securities Regulation Law Journal	Sec. Reg. L.J.
Seton Hall Constitutional Law Journal	Seton Hall Const. L.J.
Seton Hall Journal of Sport Law	Seton Hall J. Sport L.

Seton Hall Law Review	Seton Hall L. Rev.
Seton Hall Legislative Journal	Seton Hall Legis. J.
Sherbrooke Law Review	Sherbrooke. L. Rev.
Simon's Tax Cases	Simon's Tax C.
Singapore Academy of Law Annual Review	Sing. Ac. L. Ann. Rev.
Singapore Academy of Law Journal	Sing. Ac. L.J.
Singapore Journal of International & Comparative Law	Sing. J.I.C.L.
Singapore Journal of Legal Studies	S.J.L.S.
Singapore Law Review	Sing. L. Rev.
Singapore Year Book of International Law	S.Y.B.I.L.
SMU Law Review	SMU L. Rev.
Social and Legal Studies	Soc. & Leg. Stud.
Socialist Lawyer	Sol. L.
Solicitor's Journal	Solic. J.
South African Journal on Human Rights	S.AJ.H.R.
South African Law Journal	S.African.L.J.
South African Law Reports	S. African L.R.
South African Yearbook of International Law	S.AY.B. Int'l L.
South Carolina Environmental Law Journal	S.C. Envtl. L.J.
South Carolina Law Review	S.C.L. Rev.
South Dakota Law Review	S.D.L. Rev.
South Teaxas Law Review *(formerly South Texas Law Journal)*	S. Tex. L. Rev.
Southern California Interdisciplinary Law Journal	S. Cal. Interdisciplinary L.J.
Southern California Law Review	S. Calif. L. R.
Southern California Review of Law and Women's Studies	S. Cal. Rev. L. & Women's Stud.
Southern California Sports & Entertainment Law Journal	S. Cal. Sports & Ent. L.J.
Southern Illinois University Journal	S.Ill. U.L.J.
Southern University Law Review	S.U.L. Rev.
Southwestern Journal of Law & Trade in the Americas	Sw. J. Trade Am.
Southwestern University Law Review	Sw. U.L. Rev.
Space Policy	Space Pol'y
Special Lectures of the Law Society of Upper Canada	Spec. Lect. L.S.U.C.
Sports Lawyers Journal	Sports Law. J.
St. Louis University Law Journal	St. Louis. U. L.J.
St. Louis - Warsaw Transatlantic Law Journal	St. Louis. Warsaw - Trans. L.J.

Standard Environmental Law Journal	Stan. Envtl. L.J.
Standard Journal of International Law	Stan. J. Int'l L.
Stanford Journal of Law, Business & Finance	Stan. J.L. Bus. & Fin.
Stanford Journal of Legal Studies	Stan. J.Legal Stud.
Stanford Law & Policy Review	Stan. L. & Pol'y Rev.
Stanford Law Review	Stan. L. Rev.
Stanford Technology Law Review	Stan Tech. L. Rev.
Statute Law Review	Stat. L. Rev.
Studia Canonica	Stud. Canon.
Suffolk Journal of Trial & Appellate Advocacy	Suffok J. Trial & Appellate Advoc.
Suffolk Transational Law Review *(formerly Suffolk Transatinal Law Journal)*	Suffolk Transnat'l L. Rev.
Suffolk University Law Review	Suffolk U.L. Rev.
Supreme Court Economic Review	Sup. Ct. Econ. Rev.
Supreme Court Review	Sup. Ct. Rev.
Supreme Court Economic Review	Sup. Ct. Econ. Rev.
Supreme Court Law Review	Sup. Ct. L. Rev.
Sydney Law Review	Sydney L.R.
Syracuse Journal of International Law & Commerce	Syracuse J. Int'l L. & Com.
Syracuse Law Review	Sayracuse L. Rev.
Syracuse University Law and Technology Journal	Syracuse U.L. & T.J.
Tax Law Review	Tax L. Rev.
Taxettin International	Tax. Intl'l.
Telecommunications & Space Journal	Telecom. & Space J.
Temple Environmental Law & Technology Journal	Temp. Envtl. L. & Tech. J.
Temple International & Comparative Law Journal	Temp. Int'l & Comp. L.J.
Temple Law Review *(formerly Temple Law Quarterly)*	Temp. L. Rev.
Temple Political & Civil Rights Law Review	Temp. Pol. & Civ. Rts. L. Rev.
Tennessee Law Review	Ten. L. Rev.
Texas Bar Journal	Tex. B.J.
Texas Forum on Civil Liberties & Civil Rights	Tex. F. On C.L. & C.R.
Texas Hispanic Journal of Law & Policy *(formerly Hispanic Law Journal)*	Tex Hispanic J.L. & Pol'y
Texas Intellecutal Property Law Journal	Tex. Int'l L.J.
Texas Journal of Business Law	Tex. J. Bus. L.
Texas Journal of Women & the Law	Tex J. Women & L.

Texas Law Review	Tex. L. Rev.
Texas Review of Law & Politics	Tex. Rev. L. & Pol.
Texas Tech. Law Review	Tex. Tech. L. Rev.
Texas Wesleyan Law Review textes adoptes par I'Assemblee (Conseil de I'eupore)	Tex. Wesleyan L. Rev.
Textes Adoptes	Texts Adopted
Theoretical Inquiries in Law	Theor. Inq. L.
Third World Legal Studies	Third World Legal Stud.
Thomas Jefferson Law Review	Thomas Jefferson L. Rev.
Thomas M. Cooley Journal of Practical & Clinical Law	T.M. Cooley J. Prac. & Clinical L.
Thomas M. Cooley Law Review	T.M. Cooley L. Rev.
Thurgood Marshall Law Review	T. Marshall L. Rev.
Tilburg Foreign Law Review	Tilburg Foreign L. Rev.
Toledo Journal of Great Lakes' Law, Science & Policy	Tol. J. Great Lakes' L. Sci. & Pol'y
Tolley's Communications Law	Tolley's Comm. L.
Tort & Insurance Law Journal	Tort & Ins. L.J.
Touro Environmental Law Journal	Touro Envtl. L.J.
Touro Internastional Law Review	Touro Int'l L. Rev.
Touro Law Review	Touro L. Rev.
Trade Law Topics	Trade L. Topics
Transnational Law & Contemporary Problems	Transnat'l L. & Contemp. Probs.
Transnational Lawyer	Transnat'l Law.
Transportation Law Journal	Transp.L.J.
Travaux de I'association Henri Capitant dfes amis de las culture juridique frncaise	Travaux de I'assoc. Henri Capitant
Trent Law Journal	Trent. L.J.
Tribal Law Journal	Tribal L.J.
Tribune des droits humain	Trib. Dr. hum.
Trust Law International	Trust L. Int'l
Trusts & Estates	Trusts & Est.
Tulane Environmental Law Journal	Tul. Envtl. L.J.
Tulane European & Civil Law Forum	Tul. Eur. & Civ. L.F.
Tulane Journal of International & Comparative Law	Tul. J. Int'l & Com. L.
Tulane Journal of Law and Sexuality	Tul. J.L. & Sexuality
Tulane Law Review	Tul. L. Rev.

Tulane Maritime Law Journal	Tul. Mar. L.J.
Tulsa Journal of Comparative & International Law	Tulsa J. Com. & Int'l L.
Tulsa Law Journal	Tulsa L.J.
U.C. Davis Journal of International Law & Policy	U.C. Davis J. Int'l L. & Pol'y
U.C.Davis Law Review	U.C. Davis L. Rev.
UCLA Asian Pacific American Law Journal	UCLA Asian Pac. Am. L.J.
UCLA Bulletin of Law and Technology	UCLA Bull. L. & T.
UCLA Entertainment Law Review	UCLA Ent. L. Rev.
UCLA Journal of Environmental Law & Policy	UCLA J. Envtl. L & Pol'y
UCLA Journal of International Law and Foreign Affairs	UCLA J. Int'l & Foreign Aff.
UCLA Law Review	UCLA L. Rev.
UCLA Pacific Basin Law Journal	UCLA Pac. Basin. L.J.
UCLA Women's Law Journal	UCLA Women's L.J.
UMKC Law Review	UMKC L. Rev.
UNCTAD Law Review: Journal on Law, Trade and Development	UNCTAD L. Rev.
Uniform Commercial Code Law Journal	Unif. Comm. Code. L.J.
Uniform Law Conference of Canada: Proceeding	Unif. L. Conf. Proc.
Uniform Law Review	Unif. L. Rev.
United States – Mexico Law Journal	U.S.-Mex.L.J.
University of Arkansa at Little Rock Law Review	U. Ark. Little Rock L. Rev.
University of Baltimore Intellectual Property Law	U. Balt. Intell. Prop. L.j.
University of Baltimore Journal of Environmental Law	U. Balt. J. Envtl. L.
University of Baltimore Law Forum	U. Balt. L.F.,
University of Baltimore Law Review	U. Balt. L. Rev.
University of British Columbia Law Review	U.B.C.L. Rev.
University of California at Davis Law Review	U.C. Davis L. Rev.
University of Chicago Law Review	U. Chicago. L. Rev.
University of Chicago Law School Roundtable	U. Chicago L. Sch. Roundtable
University of Chicago Legal Forum	U. Chicago Legal F.
University of Cinicinnati Law Review	U. Cin. L. Rev.
University of Colorado Law Review	U. Colo. L. Rev.
University of Dayton Law Review	U. Dayton L. Rev.
University of Detroit Mercy Law Review	U. Det. Mercy L. Rev.
University of Dayton Law Review	U. Dayton L. Rev.

University of Detroit Mercy Law Review	U. Det. Mercy L. Rev.
University of Florida Journal of Law & Public Policy	U. Fl. J.L. & Pub. Pol'y
University of Ghana Law Journal	U.G.L.J.
University of Hawaii Law Review	U Haw. L. Rev.
University of Illinois Law Review	U. Ill. L. Rev.
University of Kansas Law Review	U. Kan. L. Rev.
University of Malaya Law Reivew	U. Mala. L. Rev.
University of Memphis Law Review	U. Mem. L. Rev.
University of Maimi Business Law Review	U. Miami Bus. L. Rev.
University of Miami Entertainment & Sports Law Review	U. Miami Ent. & Sports L. Rev.
University of Miami Inter-American Law Review (formerly University of Miami Yearbook of Internaltional Law)	U. Miami Inter-Am. L. Rev.
University of Miami Law Review	U Miami L. Rev.
University of Michigan Journal of Law Reform	U. Mich. J.L. Ref.
University of New Brunswick Law Journal	U.N.B.L.J.
University of New South Wales Law Journal	U.N.S.W.L.J.
University of Pennsylvania Journal of Constitutional Law	U. Pa. J. Const. L.
University of Pennsylavania Journal of International Economic Law	U. Pa. J. Int'l Econ. L.
University of Pennsylvania Journal of Labour and Employment Law	U. Pa. J. Lab. & Employment L.
University of Pennsylvania Law Review	U. Pa. L. Rev.
University of Pittsburgh Law Review	U. Pitts. L. Rev.
University of Queensland Law Journal	U.Q.L.J.
University of Richmond Law Review	U. Rich. L. Rev.
University of San. Francisco Law Review	U.S.F.L. Rev.
University of San Francisco Journal of Law and Social Challenges	U.S.F.J.L. & Soc. Challenges
University of San Franscisco Maritime Law Journal	U.S.F. Mar. L.J.
University of Tasmania Law Review	U. Tasm. L. Rev.
University of the District of Columbia Law Review *(formerly District of Columbia Law Review)*	U.D.C.L. Rev.
University of Toledo Law Review	U.Tol. L. Rev.
University of Toronto Faculty of Law Review	U.T. Fac. L. Rev.
University of Toronto Law Journal	U.T.L.J.
University of Western Austarila Law Review	U.W.A. L. Rev.
University of Western Ontario Law Review	U.W.O. L. Rev.

Upper Canada Law Journal	U.C.L.J.
US Supreme Court Reports	S.C.R. (U.S.)
Utah Bar Journal	Utah B.J.
Utilities Law Review	Uti. L. Rev.
Valparaiso University Law Review	Val. U.L. Rev.
Vanderbilt Journal of Entertainment Law & Practice	Vand. J. Ent. L. & Prac.
Vanderbilt Journal of Transnational Law	Vand. J. Transnat'l L.
Vanderbilt Law Review	Vand. L. R.
Vermont Bar Journal	Vt. B.J.
Vermont Law Review	Vt. L. Rev.
Victoria University of Wellingtown Law Review	V.U. W.L.R.
Vietnam Law & Legal Forum	Vietnam L. & Legal Forum
Villanova Environmental Law Journal	Vill. Envtl. L.J.
Villanova Law Review	Vill. L. Rev.
Villanova Sports and Entertainment Law Journal	Vill. Sports & Ent. L.J.
Virginia Environmental Law Journal	Va. Envtl. L.J.
Virginia Journal of International Law	Va. J. Int'l L.
Virginia Journal of Law & Technology	Va. J.L. & Tech.
Virginia Journal of Social Policy & Law	Va. J. Soc. Pol'y & L.
Virginia Journal of Sports and the Law	Va. J. Sports & L.
Virginia Law Review	Va. L. R.
Virginia Tax Review	Va. Tax Rev.
Waikato Law Review: Taumauri	Waikato L. Rev.
Wake Forest Law Review	Wake Forest L. Rev.
Waseda Bulletin of Comparative Law	Waseda Bull. Com. L.
Washburn Law Journal	Washburn L.J.
Washington & Lee Race & Ethic Ancestry Law Journal *(formerly Race & Ethic Ancestry Law Journal and Race & Ethnic Ancestry Law Digest)*	Wash. & Lee Race & Ethnic Ancestry L.J
Washington & Lee Law Review	Wash. & Lee L. Rev.
Washington Law Review	Wash. L. Rev.
Washington University Journal of Law & Policy	Wash. U.J.L. & Pol'y
Washington University Journal of Urban and Contemporary Law	Wash. U.J. Urb. & Contemp. L.
Washington University Law Quarterly	Wash. U.L.Q.
Wayne Law Review	Wayne L. Rev.
Web Journal of Current Legal Issues	Web. J.C.L.I.

West Virginia Journal of Law & Technology	W. Va. J. L. & T.
West Virginia Law Review	W. Va. L. Rev.
West. Virginia Lawyer	W. Va. Law.
West's Education Law Reporter	W. Ed. Law. Rep.
Western Law Review (San Francisco)	West. L. Rev. (SF)
Western Law Review (Canada)	West L.R. (Canada)
Western Ontario Law Review	West. Ont. L. Rev.
Western New England Law Review	W. New Eng. L. Rev.
Western State University Law Review	W. St. U.L. Rev.
Winder Journal of Public Law	Winder J. Pub. L.
Winder Law Symposium Journal	Winder L. Symp. J.
Willamette Journal of International Law & Dispute Resolution	Willamette J. Int'l. & Disp. Resol.
Williamette Law Review	Willamette L. Rev.
William & Mary Bill of Rights Journal	Wm. & Mary Bill Rts. J.
William & Mary Environmental Law & Policy Review	Wm. & Mary Envt'l L. & Pol'y Rev.
William & Mary Journal of Women and the Law	Wm. & Mary J. Women & L.
William & Mary Law Review	Wm. & Mary L. Rev.
William Mitchell Law Review	Wm. Mitchell L. Rev.
Windsor Review of Legal and Social Issues	Windsor Rev. Legal Soc. Issues
Windsor Yearbook of Access to Justice	Windsor Y.B. Access Just.
Wisconsin Environmental Law Journal	Wis. Envtl. L.J.
Wisconsin International Law Journal	Wis. Int'l L.J.
Wisconsin Law Review	Wis. L. R.
Wisconsin Women's Law Journal	Wis. Women's L.J.
Women's Rights Law Reporter	Women's Rts. L. Rep.
World Arbitration and Mediation Report	World Arb. & Mediation Rep.
World Trade and Arbitration Materials	W.T.A.M.
Wyoming Law Review (*formerly Land & Water Law Review*)	Wyo. L. Rev.
Yale Human Rights & Development Law Journal	Yale Human Rts. & Dev. L.J.
Yale Journal of International Law	Yale J. Int'l L.
Yale Journal of Law & Feminism	Yale J.L. & Feminism
Yale Journal of Law & the Humanities	Yale J.L. & Human.

Yale Journal on Regulation	Yale J. on Reg.
Yale Law & Policy Review	Yale L. & Pol'y Rev.
Yale Law Journal	Yale L.J.
Yearbook: Commercial Arbitration	Y.B. Comm. Arb.
Yearbook of Air and Space Law	Y.B. Air & Sp. L.
Yearbook of Copyright and Media Law	Y.B. Copyright & Media L.
Yearbook of European Law	Y.B. Eur. L.
Yearbook of International Law	Y.B. Int'l L.
Yearbook of International Environmental Law	Y.B. Int'l Env. L.
Yearbook of International Humanitarian Law	Y.B. Int'l Human. L.
Yearbook of Maritime Law	Y.B. Mari. L.
Yearbook of the Canadian Bar Association	Y.B.C.B.A.
Yearbook of the Europena Convention on Human Rights	Y.B. Eur. Conv. H.R.
Yearbook of the Institute of International Law	Y.B. Inst. Int'l L.
Yearbook of the International Court of Justice	Y.B.I.C.J.
Yearbook of the United Nations	Y.B.U.N.
Yearbook on Human Rights	Y.B.H.R.
Zeitschrift fur auslandisches offentliches Recht und Volkerrecht	Z.a.o.R.V.
Zeitschrift fur das gesamte Familienrecht	Fam. R.Z.
Zeitschrift fur europaisches Privatrecht	Z.Eu. P.
Zeitschrift fur Luft-Und Weltraum recht	Z.L.W.
Zeitschrift fur Rechtspolitik	Z.R.P.
Zeitschrift fur Rechtsvergleichung	Z.R.V.
Zeitschrift fur Unternehmens und Gesellschaftsrecht	Z.U.G.

BIBLIOGRAPHY

1. AALL Citation Formats Committee, *American Association Law Libraries Universal Citation Guide* (American Association of Law Libraries, 2002).
2. *AIP Style Manual* (New York: American Institute of Physics, 1990).
3. *Accessing Legal Information: Resources & Services* (Delhi: Indian Law Institute).
4. *Australian Guide to Legal Citation* (Melbourne: Melbourne University Law Review Association Inc., 2002).
5. *Canadian Guide to Uniform Legal Citation* (Scarborough, Ontario: Carswell/McGill Law Journal, 2002).
6. Dickerson, Darby. *ALWD Citation Manual: A Professional System of Citation* (Gaithersburg, MD: Aspen Publishers, 2006).
7. Dodd, Janet S. ed. *ACS Style Guide: A Manual for Authors and Editors* (Washington, D.C.: American Chemical Society, 1997).
8. Garner, Brian A. *The Elements of Legal Style* (New York: Oxford University Press, 2002).
9. Gibaldi, Joseph. ed. *MLA Style Manual and Guide to Scholarly Publishing* (New York: Modern Language Association of America, 1998).
10. Iverson, Cheryl. ed. *American Medical Association Manual of Style* (Baltimore: Williams and Wilkins, 1998).
11. Martin, Peter W. *Introduction to Basic Legal Citation* (Cornell Legal Information Institute, 2010).
12. *Oxford Standard for Citation of Legal Authorities* (Oxford: Oxford University Press, 2006).
13. Singh, Ranbir et al. *Digital Library-Legal Education and Research* (New Delhi: National Law University Press, 2010).
14. *The Bluebook: A Uniform System of Citation* (Cambridge, Mass.: Harvard Law Review Association, 2005).
15. *The Chicago Manual of Style* (Chicago: University of Chicago Press, 2003).
16. *The University of Chicago Manual of Legal Citation: The Maroonbook* (Chicago: University of Chicago Press, 2010).
17. Walker, Janice R., and Todd Taylor. *The Columbia Guide to Online Style* (New York: Columbia University Press, 1998).